In these two lectures Peter Diamond explores how time is modeled in theoretical analyses of individual industries and of an entire economy.

In the first lecture he considers equilibrium in a single market by examining the distinction between the short run and the long run in Marshallian analysis. He proposes an explicit modeling of time in place of Marshall's use of different atemporal models for different time frames. A model with different paths for different firms and models of price competition with incomplete information are presented. Data on job creation and destruction and data on price changes are examined.

In the second lecture he turns to models of an entire economy, and begins by considering how and why models of an entire economy should differ from models of a single industry. Both cyclical and seasonal data on the behavior of macro-economies are examined. The Arrow–Debreu and Hicksian ISLM models are compared with explicit-time models of the command over purchasing power.

Professor Diamond ends by indicating a direction for future research that might yield a more integrated economics.

T0318156

CHURCHILL LECTURES IN ECONOMICS

ON TIME

Frontispiece: Harold Lloyd in the film *Safety Last*
(courtesy Kobal)

ON TIME

LECTURES ON MODELS OF EQUILIBRIUM

PETER A. DIAMOND

Massachusetts Institute of Technology

CAMBRIDGE UNIVERSITY PRESS
Cambridge, New York, Melbourne, Madrid, Cape Town, Singapore, São Paulo, Delhi

Cambridge University Press
The Edinburgh Building, Cambridge CB2 8RU, UK

Published in the United States of America by Cambridge University Press, New York

www.cambridge.org
Information on this title: www.cambridge.org/9780521119764

First published 1994
This digitally printed version 2009

A catalogue record for this publication is available from the British Library

Library of Congress Cataloguing in Publication data
Diamond, Peter A.
On time: lectures on models of equilibrium / Peter A. Diamond.
p.   cm.
Includes bibliographical references and index.
ISBN 0 521 46289 4
1. Equilibrium (Economics) – Mathematical models.
I. Title
HB145.D5   1994
339.5–dc20   94-15921   CIP

ISBN 978-0-521-46289-1 hardback
ISBN 978-0-521-11976-4 paperback

For Kate, Matt, and Andy, with love

CONTENTS

PREFACE

I have been researching the inadequacies of conventional approaches to the modeling of time since 1968. My dissatisfaction with treatments of tâtonnement stability led me to think about price adjustments in real time, with individuals aware that they are partaking in a process in real time. This approach to modeling equilibrium resulted first in my 1971 analysis of search equilibrium in a single market. Reading Mortensen (1978) made me realize the power of Poisson processes for developing tractable models of real time activities and moved my concern for real time allocation processes into a more productive phase. These lectures represent an attempt to express the image of the workings of an economy that lies behind much of my research. Being invited to give these lectures pushed me into a reflection on modeling that would not have occurred otherwise.

The book is divided into two lectures; each lecture is divided into two chapters. In the lecture about individual industries, I begin by considering explicit modeling of time in a competitive setting where investment and production are the only decisions by firms; the Walrasian auctioneer handles prices. The thrust of the lecture is how atemporal modeling is (and must be) informed by explicit-time thinking and modeling. This is illustrated by a model with uncertainty about the production costs of individual firms and is argued by consideration of data on gross and net employment flows. The second chapter moves beyond this structure by recognizing price setting as a control variable of individual suppliers, dropping the fiction of the Walrasian auctioneer. Consideration of price setting leads one to models of monopolistic competition and of limited information about prices and trading opportunities. Reviewing the behavior of prices over time illuminates the kind of model we need.

The second lecture considers how a model of an entire economy needs to be more than a model of a single industry. Again, there are two chapters. The first considers general modeling questions and evidence on the behavior of entire economies over time. The second considers atemporal and explicit-time models of an entire economy, with a focus on the acquisition of purchasing power.

ACKNOWLEDGMENTS

This book is an expanded version of two lectures presented on May 4 and 5, 1993 at Cambridge and interestingly discussed by Jim Mirrlees on May 6. I am grateful for having had the opportunity to give the lectures, and for the pleasure of spending time at Churchill College again. Cambridge in May can be wonderful, and was. Frank Hahn was the perfect host.

These lectures reflect a large debt to my continuing collaborator, Olivier Blanchard. His valiant efforts to teach me macroeconomics have had mixed success, as shown in these lectures. I have also received valuable comments on earlier drafts from Daron Acemoglu, Abhijit Banerjee, Roland Bénabou, Ricardo Caballero, Stan Fischer, Harry Gakidis, Frank Hahn, Matthew Rabin, Bernie Saffran, Lones Smith, Bob Solow, Nick Stern, and Peter Temin. Helen Dippold has handled details of the manuscript with initiative, accuracy, and cheerfulness.

I also want to thank the National Science Foundation, not only for support while writing this book, but also for support when I researched the various topics that this book attempts to address.

LECTURE 1

MODELING AN INDUSTRY

CHAPTER 1

SHORT RUN AND LONG RUN

In the Preface to the first edition of his *Principles of Economics*, Alfred Marshall refers to the "element of Time" as "the centre of the chief difficulty of almost every economic problem" (1948, p. ii). I share Marshall's view of time as a source of difficulty. The picture of Harold Lloyd conveys my image of a theorist grappling with the modeling of time. In these lectures, I will examine how time is modeled in various economic analyses. My focus will be on the modeling of equilibrium, particularly equilibrium with many economic agents.[1] I will present a leisurely tour through some economic analyses, with an eye on their treatment of time. The first lecture considers models of a single industry; the second, models of an entire economy. My hope is that economic analyses will improve from awareness of the link between how time is modeled and some of the conclusions reached by the models.

1.1 Short run and long run

In Book V of his *Principles*, Marshall considers equilibrium. Let me quote a summary paragraph:

> [M]arkets vary with regard to the period of time which is allowed to the forces of demand and supply to bring themselves into equilibrium with one another, as well as

---

[1] There is a richness in the treatment of time in pairwise models, whether contract theory or game theory, which is not present in treatments of coordination with large numbers. This includes, for example, reliance, renegotiation, information arrival. Similarly, there is a significant time dimension in some attempts to develop more realistic models of individual choice (e.g., Ainslie (1992), Strotz (1955), Schelling (1984), and the collection edited by Loewenstein and Elster (1992)).

with regard to the area over which they extend. And this element of Time requires more careful attention just now than does that of Space. For the nature of the equilibrium itself, and that of the causes by which it is determined, depend on the length of the period over which the market is taken to extend. We shall find that if the period is short, the supply is limited to the stores which happen to be at hand: if the period is longer, the supply will be influenced, more or less, by the cost of producing the commodity in question; and if the period is very long, this cost will in its turn be influenced, more or less, by the cost of producing the labour and the material things required for producing the commodity. These three classes of course merge into one another by imperceptible degrees. (1948, p. 330)

This distinction among temporary, short- and long-period equilibria is familiar and is a staple of textbooks. Marshall defined them as follows:

Marginal title: Classification of problems of value by the periods to which they refer.

Four classes stand out. In each, price is governed by the relations between demand and supply. As regards *market* prices, Supply is taken to mean the stock of the commodity in question which is on hand, or at all events "in sight." As regards *normal* prices, when the term Normal is taken to relate to *short* periods of a few months or a year, Supply means broadly what can be produced for the price in question with the existing stock of plant, personal and impersonal, in the given time. As regards *normal* prices, when the term Normal is to refer to *long* periods of several years, Supply means what can be produced by plant, which itself can be remuneratively produced and applied within the given time; while lastly, there are very gradual or *Secular* movements of normal price, caused by the gradual growth of knowledge, of population, and of capital, and the changing conditions of demand and supply from one generation to another. (1948, pp. 378–9)

Marshall states clearly and convincingly why he feels the need to divide the analysis into separate considerations of different lengths of time:

The element of time is a chief cause of those difficulties in economic investigations which make it necessary for man with his limited powers to go step by step; breaking up a complex question, studying one bit at a time, and at last combining his partial solutions into a more or less complete solution of the whole riddle. ... The more the issue is thus narrowed, the more exactly can it be handled: but also the less closely does it correspond to real life. Each exact and firm handling of a narrow issue, however, helps towards treating broader issues, in which that narrow issue is contained, more exactly than would otherwise have been possible. With each step ... exact discussions can be made less abstract, realistic discussions can be made less inexact than was possible at an earlier stage. (1948, p. 366)

Marshall recognized a difficulty in his division of time in that long-period analysis does not produce a theory of actual prices. Instead, as quoted above, he referred to the prices generated by long-period analysis as normal prices, and normal prices need not equal average prices over any particular interval:

Thus we may emphasize the distinction already made between the average price and the normal price. An average may be taken of the prices of any set of sales extending over a day or a week or a year or any other time: or it may be the average of many such averages. But the conditions which are normal to any one set of sales are not likely to be exactly those which are normal to the others: and therefore it is only by accident that an average price will be a normal price; that is, the price which any one set of conditions tends to produce. In a stationary state alone, as we have just seen, the term normal always means the same thing: there, but only there, "average price" and "normal price" are convertible terms. (1948, p. 372)

To see what has become of the distinction between short and long runs, let me summarize the presentation of this issue in David Kreps' recent textbook, from which I taught this winter. Like Marshall, Kreps identifies three different models, although his trichotomy is different from Marshall's:

We imagine that firms begin with some initial levels of the factor inputs, some of which can be adjusted in the "short run," while others can only be adjusted in the "intermediate run."

Breaking time in this fashion, into a short run and an intermediate run and then partitioning the factor inputs into those that are short-run adjustable and others that are intermediate-run adjustable is hardly realistic. It would be more realistic to suppose that some of the firms can change the levels of all their factor inputs quickly, while others may be able to change very little until a lot of time has elapsed. Still, we explore what will happen in this market in the short and in the intermediate run, assuming that these time frames are meaningful and apply to all firms in the industry, and assuming that what is fixed in the short run for one firm is fixed in the short run for all. (1990, p. 269)

We continue to elaborate the theory by adding a long-run time frame ... In the long run, firms can enter and/or leave this industry: Firms that are in the industry are assumed to depart if at equilibrium prices they are sustaining losses. And firms will enter the industry if at equilibrium prices they can make strictly positive profits. (1990, p. 271)

In other words, Marshall identified a very short run where the supplies on hand were given – a vertical supply curve. He recognized that such a period might not have great relevance for storable items. Kreps skips this period and moves into a discussion where the number of firms is given, but there are different cost curves, depending on the set of adjustable factors, as opposed to historically given factors.

Thus, in approaching the modeling of time, the first step in both Marshall and Kreps is to distinguish the time frames for which the models are relevant. The second step in both books is then to use atemporal models. That is, in neither the long-run nor the short-run model does time enter explicitly. Instead, a model in which time does not appear explicitly is made to refer to different time frames by adjusting the range of allowed behaviors of economic agents. The short-run model differs from the long-run model by having fewer variables (and more parameters). In this way, we accommodate Marshall's "limited powers" of human analysis.

For Marshall, the different periods are devices for

simplified mathematical analysis of different factors affecting equilibrium. That is, simple models are used to illustrate how economic forces work. A short-run model is meant to describe how the levels of variable inputs respond to a change in circumstances that happened very shortly before the time being analyzed. A long-run model is meant to describe how slow-moving variables respond to changed circumstances that happened considerably before the time being analyzed.[2] Both models are pedagogic about forces. In this sense, neither model is about equilibrium – both models are about the working of forces.[3] While such an interpretation of the models is possible, it tends to defeat the purpose of building equilibrium models, which is to incorporate the feedback elements in the examination of the response of a system to circumstances.

An alternative way to think about these models, and one that probably reflects how people use the models in thinking about the economy, is that the models are meant to be models about equilibrium. More specifically, the models are about changes in equilibrium–comparative statics. From this perspective the short-run model is meant to answer the question of how equilibrium will change a short while after a (sort-of-permanent) change in some

[2] Difficulty in analyzing processes where different factors move at different speeds is not unique to economics. For example, Andrew Solow (1991) has written: "In order to model climate realistically, it is necessary to couple the ocean and the atmosphere into an overall model. The main difficulty in doing so arises from the great disparity between atmospheric time scales (on the order of one day) and oceanic time scales (on the order of one year to one millennium). So-called synchronously coupled ocean-atmosphere models are prohibitively time-consuming to run except with an unrealistic atemporal ocean model. Various tricks have been employed to use asynchronous coupling as a way of accelerating convergence, but the problem remains unsolved" (p. 15).

[3] With this interpretation, thinking about the economy requires the intuitive combination of several simple models. One of the great difficulties in economic analysis is the process of going from abstract analysis to thinking about the economy. That is, how does one use what one has learned from abstract analysis. The easy way out is to take the model literally. Sometimes, this seems to be what is meant by taking a model seriously. To me, taking a model seriously means putting in the effort to think through what lessons from the model one wants to take along when thinking about the economy.

parameter. Similarly, the long-run model is meant to describe how equilibrium will be different a long time after a change in some parameter.

In this setting, one can ask about the omissions (and possibly errors) from the way that time is treated. In fact, both short-run and long-run factors are working all the time. Does it matter that firms are continuously entering and exiting in trying to understand the short-run response of equilibrium? Does it matter that there are repeated short-run shocks when thinking about the long run of an industry? (This question might be phrased as asking about the difference between Marshall's normal price and Marshall's average price.) Are there questions that are omitted because of the usual way the analysis is divided into tractable parts?

As a contrast with this familiar use of atemporal models with different constraints, I want to present a model with explicit consideration of time. Since I am not trying to answer some particular question, but just trying to indicate how the analysis flows differently (gives different answers, directs attention to different research questions), I will use a simple model of these same phenomena. The ingredients I want to emphasize are explicit treatment of time, repeated occurrence of random events, and constant presence of both output adjustment by individual firms and entry and exit of firms.

But this choice of ingredients raises another issue in Marshall's analysis. Marshall relies on a further analytic simplification in long-period analysis by the use of the "representative firm." That is, Marshall felt that it was adequate to ignore the patterns of growth and decline of individual firms:

> At any particular moment some businesses will be rising and others falling: but when we are taking a broad view of the causes which govern normal supply price, we need not trouble ourselves with these eddies on the surface of the great tide. (1948, p. 378)

> Let us call to mind the "representative firm"... let us assume that the normal supply price of any amount of that

commodity may be taken to be its normal expenses of production...by that firm. (1948, p. 342)

I will follow a modeling strategy that implies dropping the representative firm as used by Marshall. Thus I am asking about the importance of what Marshall called the "eddies" when one is thinking about events that will occur some time in the future. First I will describe a simple example of a model that tries to come to grips with some of the issues of modeling time explicitly. Then I will turn to empirical work to underscore the importance of simultaneous consideration of these different factors.

1.2 Job creation and job destruction

I turn now to a simple model where firms have different (and stochastic) experiences, although the industry as a whole has a determinate equilibrium. The model is a simplified version of models developed by Boyan Jovanovic (1982) and S.A. Lippman and R.P. Rumelt (1982).[4] The model will give an example of how short-run uncertainties are important for long-run equilibrium and of how the long-run entry and exit factors can dominate short-run responses.

Entry

If we are to construct a model with explicit time, we need to consider the modeling of the set of potential firms available at any point in time. That is, in a timeless model, there is assumed to be some set of potential entrants. In the short-run model above, the set was empty. In the long-run model, there was some set of potential firms, perhaps all identical. In an explicit-time model, we need to consider

---

[4] For an extensive discussion of competitive equilibrium with uncertainty and irreversible investment, see Dixit and Pindyck (1994). For another model of continuous job creation and job destruction, but coming from continuous technical progress, see Caballero and Hammour (forthcoming). That paper, like this presentation, considers the behavior of entry and exit in response to fluctuations in industry demand.

the availability of potential entrants at each point in time. This involves answering two questions. One is whether the flow of new potential entrants is made up of ex ante identical firms. The second is whether a potential entrant that does not enter continues to be available in the future. That is, do we model potential entrants as a repeated flow or as a stock that grows when actual entry is below the flow of potential entry. The stock model has considerable appeal, particularly if combined with the disappearance of some of the potential entrants who do not enter. For simplicity, however, I will use the alternative assumption of a flow of potential entrants, who disappear from the model if they do not enter in the period in which they become available.

Since it seems realistic and is important for the analysis, I will assume an upward sloping supply curve of potential entrants. That is the expected rate of profit needed to induce entry will vary across potential firms. To begin, I will focus on steady-state models, and then consider time-varying models that preserve the anticipated profitability of the steady state. Thus, it is easy to calculate present discounted values, without detailed concern with the formulation of expectations.

I will take the supply curve of entrants in a period as available that period in response to anticipated conditions in that period. Thus, I am modeling the entry process, from the decision to enter until actual entry, as instantaneous, with no lags associated with entry. Realistically, the process of entry takes time, with firms in the process of entering able to speed up or slow down this process. Realistic modeling would be complicated, and I make the conventional simplifying assumption.

Uniform costs

To present the basic structure, I start with a model where all firms are the same ex post. There is a supply curve, $S(k)$, of firms willing to enter if the expected present discounted value of profits exceeds their cost of entry, k. As I said, if a potential firm does not enter it disappears; potential entrants do not accumulate over time. Once a firm has paid its entry cost, it bears a cost, c, of producing one unit, which is its capacity. I will denote the price at which this unit is sold by p. Thus in a steady state, the flow of profits is $p - c$. In addition, firms face the exogenous probability a of terminating. The real discount rate is r. Thus, the expected present discounted value of profits equals $(p - c)/(r + a)$.

I denote demand for the product by $D(p)$. In steady-state equilibrium, the flow of entrants equals the flow of exits, with the level set so that the market for output clears. The stock of firms is the flow of entrants divided by the Poisson exit rate, a. Thus we have a single equilibrium equation:

$$D(p) = S[(p - c)/(r + a)]/a. \qquad (1)$$

With a downward-sloping demand and an upward-sloping supply, this steady-state equation resembles a conventional static equilibrium; price is just sufficient to cover the long-run costs of the marginal firm, $c + (r + a)k$.

Stochastic costs

I now change the model to introduce uncertainty at the level of the individual firm and to recognize that firms have different costs ex post. I restrict possible costs to two, with $c_1 < c_2$. I assume that a potential entrant does not know whether it is a high-cost or a low-cost firm until after it has paid its entry cost, k.[5] The entering firm learns instantly which type of firm it is.[6] We assume that the fraction f of entrants are high cost.

Three types of steady-state equilibria are possible. If demand is high enough, then all firms remain in production until their exogenous termination. In this case, with risk neutral firms and random costs, the equilibrium

[5] An alternative model could be built with all firms having the same cost of entry, k, but different probabilities of being a high- or low-cost firm.

[6] A more realistic dynamic could be constructed by having all firms have the same two possible levels of costs, with firms differing in how often they have high costs. Firms could then learn over time what type of firm they are. This would resemble the type of learning that has been modeled by Jovanovic.

11

condition reflects expected costs, even though firms know their actual costs when producing:[7]

$$D(p) = S[(p - fc_2 - (1-f)c_1)/(r+a)]/a. \qquad (2)$$

For this to be an equilibrium, the price must be at least as large as the high cost, c_2. In this equilibrium, price is just sufficient to cover expected costs of the marginal entrant; it is not necessarily equal to the realized costs of high-cost firms. This distinction is important for selecting the atemporal Marshallian long-run model that corresponds to the equilibrium of the explicit-time model.

A second possibility is that demand is so low that high-cost firms exit without having ever produced. Thus the flow of firms that produce is $(1-f)$ times the flow of firms that pay the cost k to learn their production cost type:

$$D(p) = (1-f)S[(1-f)(p - c_1)/(r+a)]/a. \qquad (3)$$

For this to be an equilibrium, the price must be less than the high cost, c_2, and above the low cost, c_1. While all active firms have the same costs, the equilibrium price must also cover the costs of firms that exited on learning that they were high-cost firms.

The third possibility is that demand is intermediate so that high-cost firms are indifferent as to whether they remain or not. For this to be an equilibrium, the price must be exactly equal to the high cost, c_2, and the demand must lie in the range determined by having some of the high-cost firms exit voluntarily:

$$(1-f)S[(1-f)(c_2 - c_1)/(r+a)]/a < D(c_2),$$
$$D(c_2) < S[(1-f)(c_2 - c_1)/(r+a)]/a. \qquad (4)$$

For different demand levels that remain within these bounds, we have different equilibria with the same output price ($p = c_2$), but different numbers of active firms and

---

[7] The assumption of risk neutrality permits us to ignore some of the implications of missing insurance markets as well as missing contingent output markets. Obviously, we miss out on the effect of demand and cost uncertainties on the level of profitability needed to generate the equilibrium level of entry. But in order to stay focused on the modeling of time, and not on the implications of missing markets, we assume not just risk neutrality, but an accurate picture of the possibilities in the future.

thus different ratios of high-cost to low-cost firms; and different average variable costs in the industry.

The equilibrium values of the flow of new entrants and of the stock of active firms are S and D at the values shown in equation (4). In equilibrium there are $(1-f)S/a$ low-cost firms and $D-(1-f)S/a$ high-cost firms. Thus average variable cost is $\{c_1 + (c_2 - c_1)[1 - (1-f)S/(aD)]\}$. The higher the demand, the greater the number of high-cost firms, and so the greater the average variable cost in the industry. But a period of induced low demand that drives out high-cost firms does not contribute to efficiency – this market is responding efficiently to any foreseen pattern of demand.[8] That is, low demand is not a good thing because it lowers average variable cost. The flow of total costs is kS plus the flow of variable costs. Thus the flow of average total costs might rise or fall with the level of demand, depending on the sign of $ak - (1-f)(c_2 - c_1)$.

Notice that in all three types of steady state, it must be the case that exit equals entry in order to be a steady state. However, the flow of entrants and exits depends on the equilibrium price and is greater the greater the price. That is, the greater the price, the greater the expected present discounted value of profits, and so the greater the number of firms paying the cost of entry.

Varying demand

Let us consider this industry under the assumption that the demand curve has a multiplicative factor that follows a sine wave.[9] If the wave is small enough to always stay in the region where the price is equal to c_2, then variation in

---

[8] Costs have been modeled in a way that leaves no room for "slack." If there were slack and if a fall in demand led to an increase in investments (managerial time to reorganize for greater efficiency) to reduce slack, then there would be changes in X-efficiency. If firms were not cost minimizing in the decision as to the level of slack, then there could be efficiency gains from such competitive pressures.

[9] This does raise the question of the assumption of non-storable output. The alternative assumption of storability would lead us into the dynamics of inventories. In addition, the response to a known cycle is plausibly different from the response to an uncertain cycle once one introduces some (realistic) reasons for risk aversion.

demand is fully accommodated by variation in exits, with no variation in entry or in price. In other words, demand fluctuation is fully accommodated by job destruction, with no variation in job creation. Movement of demand over a wider interval so that prices varied would result in variation in entry as well. Variation in prices would happen in a model with a continuous distribution of variable costs, rather than the two-point distribution which simplifies this model so much.

Variation in prices introduces further complications for forward-looking firms. Assuming that continued production is the optimal way to continue the existence of the firm, high-cost firms are willing to bear short-run losses since they value the opportunity of possibly still existing when demand rises again. Moreover, the entry decision must recognize the possibility that good times may return. But these modifications do not alter the basic pattern of results.[10]

It is certainly possible to construct an atemporal model of a period where the price is equal to the cost of high-cost firms, with an infinitely elastic supply curve coming from exits by some of the high-cost firms. Such an approach has several shortcomings as a research strategy (although not necessarily as an accurate description). Such a model would require abandoning the normal short-period assumption of a fixed number of firms. Second, in a more general version of such a model, exit is driven not just by current prices, but also by expectations of future prices. While one can incorporate given expectations into the supply of exit, one would want to track the model over time to examine the relationship between current supply as a function of expectations of the future and the future evolution of the model. Especially if one were to impose

---

[10] To simplify the model (and be more realistic), we could assume that firms can pay a flow cost to remain in existence without actually producing. That is, we could allow firms to mothball their production capacity. Then the relationship between price and production is as described above, with varying numbers of inactive firms adjusting to the prospects of recovery. Since the Davis–Haltiwanger numbers to be described below refer to numbers of production workers, it does not distinguish between exits and shutdowns.

rational expectations, one would need the model of the future for which the expectations were rational. Even without such a sharp assumption, it is natural to want to examine the relationship between expectations and future behavior of equilibrium.

Extensions

In addition to a predictable cycle, such as the one just analyzed, we can consider a once-and-for-all shock to plot the difference between short- and long-run responses. The response to small shocks is easy to examine. With an unexpected permanent small drop in demand there is an immediate discrete lump of exiting high-cost firms so that the industry adapts instantly to the situation. A more realistic phased response would have firms slowly realizing that demand had fallen permanently. One could create a signal extraction problem to have this result. An interesting version of this model would have differing costs for different firms so that the possibility of future profits would induce some firms with short-run losses to remain in existence in the hope of a future price increase. While firms were learning about the permanence of the fall in demand, price would be lower than otherwise, slowing the rate of entry of new firms.

In contrast, a sudden rise in demand would raise price, even if it was in the range where the long-run equilibrium has no change in price. Since entry is a flow in continuous time, it takes a discrete length of time for sufficient entry (which happens at a higher rate than previously since price is higher) to drive price back to the previous level. During this period there would be no exit, other than involuntary closures from the Poisson death process. Thus the asymmetry in speed between entry and exit gives different short-run responses to increases and decreases in demand.[11]

---

[11] There are a variety of ways that the time structure of both entry and the growth of a pool of potential entrants could be varied. Entry might take time. A simple version of this model would create a pool of firms attempting to enter, with Poisson entry from this pool. That would

The articles I drew on for this simplified model were constructed to examine diverse experiences of firms. The model here has been simplified to a single source of difference, the one-time random cost draw. To pursue this model into a richer picture of firm experience, one would want a more general technology than a simple zero-one choice. One would also want repeated-cost shocks to individual firms.[12] But this would lead us astray from our focus on equilibrium.

Implications

I started by reminding you of the familiar atemporal short- and long-run Marshallian models. I then introduced a model set in real time. There are a variety of contrasts between these two approaches. The explicit-time model has simultaneous entry and exit, and so much larger gross flows of jobs than net flows. As we will see in a moment, this is true of US industries. Moreover, the model structure implied different roles for entry and exit in response to a change in demand. This is relevant for the movement of prices as demand levels vary.

When constructing atemporal models, we usually discuss time structures as part of the justification for the particular atemporal model chosen. Using an explicit-time model can be seen as a way of thinking about time so that the atemporal model has the same properties as the explicit-time one. That is, thinking in explicit time and the simplicity of atemporal modeling can be combined, provided one doesn't fall into the trap of taking the timing relations in the atemporal model literally. Basing the

---

slow entry even more relative to shocks. Second, we could allow some accumulation of potential entrants that do not choose to attempt to enter (or simply enter in the simpler version). The pool could shrink by Poisson attrition, leaving a finite available response to shocks. One could add a decision on the optimal time to enter, given expectations about future market conditions. It does seem appropriate to model entry and exit as processes with different speeds.

[12] One could interpret the Poisson arrival, a, of the exogenous closing of firms as a cost shock.

atemporal model on an explicit-time model is one way of guarding against this problem.

As one example, the short-run cost uncertainties for individual firms were seen to be important for long-run equilibrium. Thus, we can think of the explicit-time model as helping to select the right long-run atemporal model. Turning to some sort of medium run, the short-run responses of entry and exit have implications for the mix of high- and low-cost firms, and so the response of equilibrium to further changes in demand. The internal logic of pursuing such a model also leads one to research questions that one might not be led to by the pair of atemporal models.

Data

I turn now to some of the evidence supporting a picture of industry behavior with much larger gross than net flows and with continuous entry and exit. For this I turn to the empirical work of Steven Davis and John Haltiwanger (1990, 1992) on job creation and job destruction. Davis and Haltiwanger focus on employment rather than output. But there is an implicit link between the two that connects their work with the models at hand. They examine employment data at the plant level.[13] That is, they do not follow individual workers, but follow the number of employees of a plant on the day of the month when the count is made.[14] They do matching calculations based on the March to March changes as well as on quarter to quarter changes.

The data that they examine cover the period from 1972 to 1988. The data source is the Longitudinal Research

---

[13] Davis and Haltiwanger have examined this plant employment data in two publications (1990, 1992). They are also at work on a Census Bureau Monograph on this subject (together with Scott Schuh). The quinquennial plant employment data have been analyzed by Dunne, Roberts, and Samuelson (1989).

[14] For a complementary examination of labor market flows based on interviews with workers, see Blanchard and Diamond (1989, 1990a, 1990b). The pictures arising from the worker and the job sides are broadly consistent.

Database of the US Bureau of the Census. The universe being considered is manufacturing establishments with at least five employees. An establishment is a single location, a single plant (rather than a firm). Every five years, there is a full census of all these establishments. From this census, a sample is drawn that is repeatedly interviewed over the five years beginning two years after the census. New establishments are added to the sample to represent entry and to preserve a representative sample. In 1977, for example, the sample included roughly 70,000 out of the universe of roughly 360,000. Since the probability of being selected varied with size (with all establishments with over 250 employees included in the sample), the sampled establishments accounted for 76 percent of manufacturing employment. (Sample weights are used to adjust the sample to reflect the population in the numbers described below.) Thus many establishments appear in successive five-year panels. An adjustment is made to try to correct for the data difference in the first quarter of a new sample.

Each quarter, the sampled firms are asked to report the number of production workers then employed. Comparing two successive quarters, Davis and Haltiwanger divide firms into four categories. Entrants are firms that have employees in the second observation, but not in the first. The contribution of entry to the employment change is the sum of employment levels over all firms that are new entrants. Similarly, we have firms with positive employment in the first quarter, but none in the second. These are exits and the sum over such establishments is the contribution of exits to the employment changes. For firms that have positive employment at both observations, Davis and Haltiwanger divided the sample into those that had employment growth and those that had employment decline. Summing the employment changes over the establishments with growth and over those with declines, we have expansions and contractions. Job creation is the sum of employment growth from entry and from expansion. Job destruction is the sum of employment changes from contractions and exits. For the annual data, they compare total employment (not just production workers) at the plant level from the pay period containing March 12 of one year to the one containing March 12 of the following year.[15]

The data are clear on the vastly larger size of gross than net flows. In the annual data, on average over this period (1972–88), 10.1 percent of manufacturing jobs are destroyed in a one-year period.[16] Yet over the period, the average rate of decline of manufacturing jobs was 1.1 percent. The difference is accounted for by a job creation rate of 9.1 percent. At a quarterly rate, the job destruction rate was 5.5 percent, the job creation rate was 5.2 percent, and net employment decrease was 0.3 percent. Thus the picture of much larger gross than net flows is accurate. Davis and Haltiwanger cite data from Canada, France, Germany, Israel, Italy, and Sweden that show a similar picture. They also report that there is a great deal of persistence in the gross changes at the plant level. That is, an increase in employment at a plant is likely to result in a continued higher level of employment for some time thereafter, with a parallel result for a decrease.[17]

Davis and Haltiwanger also report on job creation and job destruction divided up among changes of different percentage sizes. At an annual frequency, on average,

[15] Note that the measurement is a comparison of employment levels at two dates. Thus a temporary layoff followed by a recall that happens between the two observations is not a destroyed job. A temporary layoff between observations, followed by a recall after the second does register as a destroyed job. Similarly, a quit leaving a vacancy that is not yet filled at the time of the second observation is also a destroyed job. Given the speed with which jobs are filled, in all but the tightest labor markets, this effect is unlikely to be important.

[16] For the denominator for percentage calculations, Davis and Halti-wanger use the average of employment in the two periods being compared.

[17] Using quarterly data, on average, 72 percent of jobs created in quarter t are still there in quarter $t + 1$; 59 percent of jobs created in quarter t are still there in quarters $t + 1$ and $t + 2$; 40 percent in all quarters up to $t + 4$; 26 percent in all quarters up to $t + 8$. For job destruction, these percentages are 75 percent, 64 percent, 51 percent, and 44 percent. Using annual data, between 60 percent and 73 percent of jobs created in particular years were still present a year later; between 43 percent and 58 percent were present both one and two years later. For job destruction, the ranges of values were 72 percent to 88 percent and 62 percent to 82 percent.

plant shutdowns account for 23 percent of job destruction, while plant startups account for 16 percent of job creation. At a quarterly frequency, these percentages are naturally smaller, being 12 percent and 8 percent. Since, on average, net employment decreases were less than 6 percent of job destruction, employment loss from shutdowns exceeded the net employment loss. Thus exits are sufficiently important to belong in a model addressing a period as short as a quarter. Beyond the importance of complete shutdowns and startups, large percentage changes are also important. For example, at a quarterly frequency, an additional 19 percent of job creation was in plants that were in existence at the first date and at least doubled in size. Similarly, an additional 21 percent of job destruction was in plants where employment fell by at least half and the plants continued to produce. Thus large changes were 25–30 percent of gross changes and four to five times net changes.

Davis and Haltiwanger reach several other conclusions about employment change patterns. One is that the concentration of job destruction in large changes is larger than the concentration of job creation in large changes. (Exit is more concentrated than entry.) Secondly, they examine the behavior of both job creation and destruction over the business cycle. Not surprisingly, there are large cyclical movements in both measures. Interestingly, job destruction shows considerably higher cyclical responsiveness than job creation. Thus gross reallocation, defined as the sum of creation and destruction is larger in recessions than in booms.[18] That the model I presented above has this property is not totally coincidental. Nor is the property of the model that changes in quantities can be large without large changes in prices.

In this chapter, we have examined the timing of entry and exit and the time structure of learning about uncertainty in determining equilibrium levels of investment and production. These issues need to be considered

---

[18] Davis and Haltiwanger also do their analysis at the industry level as well as at the level of total manufacturing, and, exploiting the longitudinal nature of the data, consider events separately at plants of different ages, as well as of different sizes.

in selecting an atemporal model to approximate long-run equilibrium. These issues also implied a sensitivity of the short-run atemporal model to the makeup of the industry (mix of low- and high-cost firms, expectations of future profitability). In addition, this approach focused attention on medium-run issues where one follows the evolution of short-run responses as a consequence of the endogenously varying makeup of the industry. We saw that the explicit modeling of time is not only an interesting theoretical strategy for combining various economic forces and time frames, but also resulted in a model that represents a much closer first approximation to the actual behavior of manu-facturing industries.

Apart from the two elements examined, the models used standard competitive assumptions. Thus issues of com-mitment and coordination, both of which have important time dimensions, were ignored. The next chapter goes further in the exploration of the timing of behavior and of information, with a focus on prices rather than quantities.

CHAPTER 2

PRICING

Both the atemporal Marshallian analysis and the explicit-time entry–exit model discussed in chapter 1 had the same interaction between demand and supply within a period. With the time structure implicit in this modeling, any attempt to charge more than the "market price" fails completely, while the entire market can be taken by a price below the market price. Thus an instant response by demanders to any variation in pricing behavior is implicitly assumed. This is a common strategy for model simplification: one action happens infinitely more rapidly than another. Once we start paying attention to how long it takes to learn things and to do things, this assumption becomes implausible for many markets.

Marshall identified both space and time as issues in the analysis of a market. In his analysis of sticky prices, Robert Gordon (1981) has argued that some commodity allocations have an important tradeoff between space and time. In markets with a single location for transactions (or a small number), prices seem to react very quickly to imbalances in desired trades. But the use of a single location makes examination and collection of physical commodities prohibitively expensive. In contrast with stock markets, grocery stores have their products available for both examination and collection at a widely dispersed set of locations. Moreover, prices within a grocery store do not behave like prices on a stock exchange. Some prices (e.g., produce) are changed frequently, but not continuously; other prices are changed infrequently. Some items are "on sale." The strategic intent of stores, along with the costs of different items are important in understanding pricing. Presumably the dispersion of market interactions over space affects the speed of general price movements.[1]

While one can think of each grocery store location as a separate Arrow–Debreu market, this loses sight of the market power of the sole supplier in each market. This market power is diluted by the presence of other grocery stores; but it is not removed. The spread of physical locations seems central for this deviation from the competitive model and leads naturally to monopolistic competitive models.

If we begin our thinking about such geographically dispersed markets by recognizing that prices are typically set by suppliers, we need to model the response of demanders to the array of (possibly different) prices being set by different suppliers. How quickly (and whether) demanders respond to differences in supplier pricing varies with the nature of demanders, and with the flow of information. In particular, one might think that a market with professionals on both sides of the market differed from one with professionals on one side and amateurs on the other. Interestingly, Marshall thought so. In a footnote in *Principles*, he wrote:

> A man may not trouble himself much about small retail purchases: he may give half-a-crown for a packet of paper in one shop which he could have got for two shillings in another. But it is otherwise with wholesale prices. A manufacturer can not sell a ream of paper for six shillings while his neighbour is selling it at five. For those whose business it is to deal in paper know almost exactly the lowest price at which it can be bought, and will not pay more than this. The manufacturer has to sell at about the market price, that is at about the price at which other manufacturers are selling at the same time. (1948, p. 328)

I read this paragraph as suggesting that Marshall considered atemporal competitive theory as relevant for

---

[1] Gordon identified five stylized facts to be explained by price adjustment theory: some prices do not change over long periods; some prices, although set on price tags, change every day; the division of nominal GNP changes between prices and quantities varies over time; and over countries; and hyperinflation is possible.

markets for intermediate products, but not for retail markets. In markets where (at least) some customers are behaving in the way described by Marshall (at least) some firms will set prices in a way that reflects the absence of complete price competition. The standard competitive model will not describe such an equilibrium. Search theory has been developed to describe equilibrium when consumers do not always find the lowest price. "Search theory" is a misnomer. In the standard competitive model, demanders always find the lowest price. When an economist objects to search theory on the grounds that he "does not search for a low price," his behavior is described more accurately by search theory than by the standard competitive model. This confusion might have been avoided if search theory had been called "costly search theory," with the standard competitive model referred to as "costless search theory."

Learning about low prices generally occurs over time, although models of equilibrium with limited information can be atemporal or set explicitly in time. Even without limited information, the ability to substitute a later purchase for a current purchase affects market power.[2] In this chapter, I will examine some models reflecting the time and resource costs associated with shopping and summarize some studies of actual price setting.

2.1 Monopolistic competition

In the conventional market setting of instantaneous response, it does not matter whether we think of suppliers as setting prices or setting quantities.[3] Once we move to a

---

[2] These lectures focus on equilibria with many suppliers. Thus I will not discuss the role of the time dimension for commitment issues. For a discussion of the role of intertemporal substitution in the dilution of monopoly power in the absence of commitment (the Coase conjecture), see Tirole (1988). Similarly, I will not discuss differences in equilibria between single period games and repeated games. Again, one can consult Tirole.

[3] In a game theoretic setting (as opposed to a competitive market model), price-setting and quantity-setting games are generally different. Even if

more realistic structure of time and space, we need to pay attention to the fact that in many retail markets it is prices that are set by suppliers, although there is some bargaining. In competitive market theory, a homogeneous commodity sells at the same price over nearby locations that form a single market. Similarly, in normal times, competitive theory would imply smoothly changing prices at nearby moments of time. Yet both of these presumptions are untrue in the US.

In a much cited paper, John Pratt, David Wise, and Richard Zeckhauser (1979) presented data from a telephone survey in the Boston area. Using the Yellow Pages, they solicited price quotations on thirty-nine commodities. They found ratios of the highest to the lowest price in excess of two to one for seventeen of these thirty-nine commodities (some homogeneous, some not). Similarly, studies of financial markets have found different interest rates in transactions that appear to be very similar. For example, James J. White and Frank W. Munger, Jr (1971) found consumers paying different interest rates for auto loans even though it appeared that some people paying high rates could have borrowed at low rates. In their study of annuities, Benjamin Friedman and Mark Warshawsky (1990) found very different internal rates of return on policies sold by different large insurance companies (although they did not examine the financial soundness of the different companies). Mutual funds vary considerably in load factors, even when they follow similar investment strategies (Forbes, February 15, 1993).

There are different ways to alter the competitive model to accommodate distributions of prices. One way focuses on "space" rather than time. Monopolistic competitive models that identify the supplies of different firms as different commodities with limited substitution fall into this category.[4] Alternatively, there is a literature that

there is a unique relationship between prices and quantities, conjecturing that others will keep prices constant is generally different from conjecturing that others will keep quantities constant.

[4] Monopolistic competitive models also address the determination of the set of available products. In an atemporal setting, the array of available

focuses on limited consumer information about prices and the availability of commodities.

One familiar model focusing on "space" is that of Steven Salop (1979) where firms are located around a circle, so that each firm has two competitors, its two neighbors around the circle that is the simplified geography of the economy. Recognizing the richness of geography (and more complicated descriptions of taste differences) it seems appropriate to consider models where each firm competes against many others, for example, as in Oliver Hart (1985). In Hart's model, each consumer obtains utility only from a subset of the goods that exist, with all consumers having a subset of the same size. The set of all consumer preferences contains all possible subsets (of the same size) of commodities as the subset of commodities that give utility. Thus each firm competes against every other firm. That is, for any pair of commodities, there is a set of consumers who like this pair. Hart studies the case where the distribution of preferences is symmetric over commodities in order to examine the limiting properties of equilibrium as the number of commodities expands without limit. Thus, no pairs of commodities are "neighbors"; all firms compete against all other firms. In practice the complexity of geography reflects combinations of these two polar cases. For example, with different people following different routes between home and work, different people face a choice from different sets of gas stations that can be visited without detours and for which prices are readily observable (although generally sequentially). But two gas stations that are side-by-side are competing for all consumers who might visit either one.

products depends on the structure of production costs, of preferences (and so demands), and on the nature of competition. There is clearly an important time dimension to this question which has been analyzed in the context of network externalities. A literature has grown up on dynamic equilibrium where such externalities are important; see, for example, Farrell and Saloner (1985) and Katz and Shapiro (1986). For the purposes of this lecture, I will concentrate on pricing behavior and ignore the issue of product design, despite the obvious importance of moving beyond atemporal models in the consideration of product design.

The monopolistic competitive model recognizes that "similar" goods frequently differ in their characteristics in ways that matter to (at least) some consumers. Moreover, the conditions of sale (such as lines at checkout counters) are also usefully considered characteristics of the goods. Thus monopolistic competition models are consistent with a distribution of prices for "similar" goods, although it would take considerable study to determine whether the degree of variation of prices is consistent with a plausible degree of differences in the commodities. In addition, monopolistic competition models are consistent with having prices generally exceed marginal costs. That prices do generally exceed marginal costs is apparent from the general eagerness of businesses to make more sales.

In this line of analysis, markups depend on demand elasticities, which, in turn, depend on the characteristics of preferences and the set of available commodities. Thus the atemporal monopolistic competitive model focuses on variation in the elasticity of demand as the central issue in determining whether markups are higher in high- or low-demand times. This model identifies some issues that are important for understanding equilibrium; but, it seems to me, the model is still missing an important factor. The need to add incomplete information about prices (or incomplete responsiveness to price differences) becomes apparent once we consider the behavior of prices over short periods of time. That is, we would expect the monopolistic competitive model to display smooth price changes unless underlying parameters changed abruptly. Yet the presence of sales implies large changes in some prices over short periods of time.

Elizabeth Warner and Robert Barsky (1993) have gathered and studied daily data on retail prices. Every day from November 1, 1987 to February 29, 1988, Warner visited seventeen stores in Ann Arbor to check the prices on a list of eight commodities. If the commodity was not in stock, she recorded the commodity as unavailable rather than as available at the listed price. She adjusted for commodities that were on sale, with a markdown available. Since not all eight commodities were carried by all seventeen stores, there were a total of 40 outlet-specific good-specific price sequences.

The findings are interesting from a number of perspectives. First they record the extent to which prices vary significantly (e.g., 10 percent off) over short periods of time because of sales, even though list prices did not vary. For thirty-one of these forty commodity–store combinations there was at least one sale in the four-month observation period, including at least one sale for each commodity. For thirteen of the commodity–store combinations there were two or more sales. Many of these are temporary markdowns and so represent two price changes. That the price returns to the same level may reflect the technology of menu costs or the complexity of the decision process.

Naturally, they found that seasonal goods, like sweaters, had price declines as the season ended. A natural question to ask is whether prices were higher when demand was high (before Christmas) or when demand had presumably declined (after Christmas). They found no single pattern. For example 45 percent of the outlet-specific commodity-specific prices were lower before Christmas, while 35 percent were lower after Christmas, and nearly 20 percent had unaltered price tags throughout the period. They also found that prices were lowest on Friday and Saturday and highest on Monday. They also found that one-third of the commodity–store combinations that ever had a markdown had one on the weekend after Thanksgiving.

Peter Pashigian and Brian Bowen (1991) have also examined sales, by examining the fraction of department store sales of shirts at markdown. They noted that a larger percentage of shirts are sold on sale from Friday to Sunday than from Monday to Wednesday.

Monopolistic competition theory would approach these findings from the perspective of demand elasticities. For example, seasonal goods may have higher demand elasticities toward the end of the season. That is, the kind of people who choose to buy late in the season may be the kind of people who find different goods closer substitutes for each other. Similarly, one could look for reasons for variation in demand elasticity across shoppers who choose to shop on different days of the week. For example, Warner and Barsky note that many working people find it more convenient to shop on the weekend (including Friday night) than during the week. This leads to greater demand in some markets on the weekend than during the week. They observe that in the Salop (1979) model of firms located around a circle, holding constant the number of (evenly spaced) firms (as is appropriate on the time scale of variation within a week), an increase in demand results in a drop in markups.

However, we also need to explain why the elasticity affects pricing by resulting in a small number of goods with significant temporary price cuts, rather than a more uniform pattern across both goods and time. All in all, reliance on monopolistic competition alone does not seem to work as a full explanation, but the central underlying observation – of elasticities reflecting preference patterns – is relevant, and is missing in models that assume homogeneous commodities as part of the model simplification strategy.

2.2 Demand uncertainty and price uncertainty

Moving away from successive (more or less) independent atemporal periods to focus on time structure, one can consider the revelation of information over time to both sellers and buyers. Suppliers may not know how much consumers value commodities until an attempt is made to sell them. We are all aware of some large failures in the introduction of new products, such as the Edsel. Generally, a large fraction of new products fail to be profitable. Some sellers of their condominiums start by asking high prices that are quickly reduced in the absence of a sale, although many people do not change their asking price, even over relatively long times.[5]

The revelation of demand uncertainty has been studied in the less dramatic setting of clothing. Edward Lazear (1986) has developed such a model and Pashigian (1988)

---

[5] Genesove and Mayer, personal communication about work in progress.

and Pashigian and Bowen (1991) have applied it to data on clothing prices.[6] In the model, it is optimal for suppliers to set high prices early in a season, before they know which items will be highly valued, and then to lower the prices of goods that do not sell as a response to the information revealed by the failure of the goods to sell. This explanation is clearly relevant for some goods, but not all, nor is it an explanation of temporary markdowns early in the season.

When intertemporal substitution is possible, consumers want to know about future prices as well as the array of current prices. If present and future prices were predictable, some consumers would wait for low prices. But if consumers do not know when the prices will be low, then we can support an equilibrium with varying prices by having a higher elasticity among those most willing to wait. Moreover, any firm contemplating a change in price needs to keep the date of the change stochastic in order to limit the shifting of demand to later lower prices. Thus equilibria with stochastic prices and equilibria with stochastic dates of price change have been studied by Hal Varian (1980) and by Roland Bénabou (1989).[7]

Demand uncertainty and prices that are set for some period of time also result in equilibria with price distributions. In the simplest version of this idea, suppliers must attach (unchangeable) prices to commodities before they know the level of aggregate demand during the period for which the stocks on hand are the only goods available. In Edward Prescott's (1975) version of this model, aggregate demand is simply uncertain and firms must price their goods before knowing aggregate demand. Prescott assumes that consumers find the lowest available prices. Thus, with uncertain aggregate demand, goods with different prices

---

[6] Pashigian and Bowen, 1992, have also examined the change in the seasonal pattern of prices for automobiles as the structure of model changes has varied.

[7] Some stores have a policy of giving rebates to a customer who purchases a good that goes on sale shortly thereafter. While this appears to be a contradiction to the modeling described in the text, I suspect that the limited number of customers who know about the policy and request the rebate preserves the relevance of the theory.

have different probabilities of sale; goods with low prices are sold whenever goods with higher prices are sold, but not vice versa. The condition of equal expected profits for different prices determines the equilibrium distribution of prices as a function of the distribution of aggregate demand.

It is not surprising to have unsold goods when prices are set before demand is known. Interestingly, as Julio Rotemberg (1988) has pointed out, one does not need to have predetermined prices for this result. Slow revelation of information can yield the same result. That is, we can model firms as following the optimal pricing strategy based on what they know as the "period" progresses, but with the assumption that they do not know total demand when carrying out early transactions. Critical for this equilibrium is the idea that firms sell to consumers at an agreed-on price, not at a price that is indexed to information that becomes available later in time. Thus firms start with a stock of inventory. Sequentially (but within a single period), customers appear to make purchases. The firm can price goods as a function of the number of sales made thus far (within the period). But when aggregate demand within the period is exhausted, remaining units remain unsold. This equilibrium with pricing strategies has the same structure as the one with price commitments. The structure represents a way of using a discrete-time model to mimic a process in continuous time. As a "sequential service constraint," it was initiated by Douglas Diamond and Philip Dybvig (1983) in their analysis of bank runs. To model this phenomenon in continuous time, one would need to consider the pattern of resupply relative to the awareness of demand changes.[8]

Thus we started with an atemporal (single period) monopolistic competitive model. We then added a time dimension to allow for different demand elasticities for people shopping in different periods. For this to work well, we added uncertainty about the timing of future price

[8] A similar issue arises in labor markets, with the setup cost of an employment relationship substituting for the cost advantages of batch ordering for retail sales.

cuts, even though individuals were informed about contemporaneous pricing. A time dimension was also used to introduce two sources of uncertainty for suppliers – the level of aggregate demand for the industry and the (relative) demand for a particular commodity.

Costly search

Switching back to the demand side, we can recognize, as Marshall did, that consumers do not know all the current market opportunities. Limited information about opportunities naturally gives market power to people trading with the ill informed.[9] One does not need to go further than being a consumer to realize the limited amount of information that we have about prices. I am not aware of much systematic work on consumer information,[10] I will assume various degrees of limited information and explore some implications for equilibrium.

Let me start with a model that reflects the self-described behavior I quoted at the start of this chapter. Assume that some consumers behave according to the competitive model, always buying at the lowest available price, while others purchase at the first store visited, a store chosen at random.[11] On the supply side, assume free entry of identical firms with U-shaped costs. Assuming sufficient consumers of each type, two pricing strategies will coexist in equilibrium. Some stores will charge the competitive price. There will be enough of these stores to service (at minimum average cost) all of the competitive customers plus the non-searching customers randomly selecting

---

[9] See, e.g., Diamond (1971).

[10] Brown and Oxenfeldt (1972) examine consumer perceptions of relative price levels in different supermarkets. Nagle and Novak (1988) examine the hypothesis that some of the variation in supermarket markups comes from pricing to affect consumer perceptions of store-wide average prices, which depends on remembered prices, which are disproportionately frequently purchased items.

[11] This structure is similar to that in Salop and Stiglitz (1977). In assuming two types of consumers who do and do not respond to incentives, I am following the approach taken by Haltiwanger and Waldman (1991).

these stores. The remaining stores will charge the monopoly price, with enough stores so that they all break even.
While there is a distribution of prices in this market,
customers who can search costlessly are not affected by the
presence of customers who do not search. But some
customers who do not search gain from the presence of
low-price stores that cater to the costless searchers.

This model has used the standard atemporal Marshallian long-run model with identical firms. One can combine
costless searchers and non-searchers, as in this model,
with high- and low-cost firms, as in the model presented in
chapter 1. This model is examined in Appendix A for
parameters that have high-cost firms indifferent to exiting.
With only a few non-searchers, the model remains as
described in chapter 1, with the price equal to the costs of
the high-cost firms. With more non-searchers, high-cost
firms are indifferent between high- and low-price strategies and some non-searchers pay a higher price. With even
more non-searchers, all high-cost firms charge a high price
and low-cost firms are indifferent between the two strategies. In this case, the presence of non-searchers harms the
costless searchers, since prices are higher in the stores
serving the costless searchers. These "pecuniary"
externalities matter for the efficiency of equilibrium.

In contrast with these models, we can consider the
model of Gerard Butters (1977), where all consumers are
the same and receive price information only from stores
engaging in advertising. Firms advertise, with different
consumers learning about different numbers of potential
sellers. Consumers have a common reservation price and
will purchase at the best price they learn of provided it is
below their reservation price. In a setting where some
consumers learn of only a single supplier, while others
learn of more than one, the only equilibrium is to have a
distribution of prices, with a range of prices extending
from the competitive price to the monopoly price.[12] At

---

[12] The reasoning behind this conclusion is the following. Consider the
possibility of an equilibrium with all prices the same. If this is at the
competitive price, there is no profit from a sale. Therefore, raising the
price (but still below the reservation price) yields a profit since there is

each price, there is equal expected profitability, combining the probability of a sale with the profit from the sale.

One can add non-searchers to this model by having some people randomly choose one of their price quotes, while others buy at the lowest available price. For a given number of ads, non-searchers lower the probability of a sale for low price ads and raise it for high price ads. Thus, as shown in Appendix B, equilibrium with non-searchers has more ads. Since the equilibrium in the Butters model is efficient, in aggregate, consumers are harmed by the presence of non-searchers.

In contrast with these two models, much of the literature focuses on the incentive for search, whether sequential search or non-sequential search. In a variety of settings, equilibrium again shows a distribution of prices.[13] All of these models show significant market power generated by limited information. In these models, we would generally expect non-searchers to have an adverse effect on costly searchers. The presence of firms pricing high for non-searchers makes the search problem of costly searchers more difficult. Moreover, this increase in the difficulty of the search problem increases the reservation prices of costly searchers, which adds to the incentive for higher prices.

In addition to price variation from the unfolding of an uncertain future, there are models of price variation associated with intertemporal links in demand or supply and variations in the level of demand. These have been devel-

---

some probability of it being the only price that some consumer learns of. If the uniform price is above the competitive price, then a firm has an incentive to lower its price infinitesimally, since that will result in an infinitesimal drop in profits should a sale be made, but a discrete increase in the probability of making a sale. Similarly, one can conclude that there are no atoms in the distribution of prices. With free entry, the lowest price must be the competitive price since at the lowest price the probability of a sale is one. Similarly, the highest price must be the reservation price since sales at the highest price are made only to consumers knowing about just one price.

[13] See, for example, Axell (1977), Bénabou, (1993), Burdett and Judd (1983), Diamond (1987), Frankel (1994), Reinganum (1979), Rob (1985), Salop and Stiglitz (1977), Shilony (1977), Wilde (1977), Wilde and Schwartz (1979).

oped with an eye on business cycle frequencies rather than shorter periods. In Edmund Phelps and Sidney Winter (1970), consumers are slow to switch suppliers in response to price differences. Thus there is a tradeoff between higher short-run profits from higher prices and lower long-run profits from a decline in market share. The balance of these forces varies with the level of current demand relative to the level of future demand. Julio Rotemberg and Garth Saloner (1986) have developed an oligopolistic model where implicit collusion is supported by a threat of price wars. Pricing is set to avoid the incentive to cheat and trigger such a war. The price that makes price cutting unattractive depends on the level of current demand relative to future demand. In this model prices are higher when demand is lower (relative to the future).[14]

We have seen that the problem of optimal pricing is a difficult one, beset with uncertainties. Thus, it is not surprising to observe complexity in pricing behavior, both by individual firms and across market settings. This is true in the type of setting we have been examining of many suppliers and so no strategic feedback. The story gets more complicated once we add such feedbacks, as is surely suitable for many markets. Another conclusion from this discussion is that prices generally exceed marginal costs, since price setters generally have some degree of market power. If prices didn't exceed marginal cost, firms would not care about making marginal sales. Yet firms generally appear quite eager to make additional sales.

2.3 Sticky prices

I have described data and models that refer to a distribution of prices at a single point in time. While I have also examined temporary markdowns, the vocabulary and

---

[14] The difficulty in measuring marginal cost makes it difficult to judge whether markups of price over marginal cost are higher in booms or recessions. For conflicting results, contrast the work of Bils (1987) and of Rotemberg and Woodford (1991) who find countercyclic markups with that of Domowitz, Hubbard, and Petersen (1988) who find procyclic markups.

focus have been on prices, not changes in prices. I want to turn now to consideration of changes in prices, both regular variation in prices and reconsideration and (possible) resetting of prices. In a way, this distinction resembles that between stocks and flows when considering quantities. My focus will be on individual prices, rather than average prices.[15]

Let us start with a familiar example – the variation of telephone charges with the time of day and the day of the week. This example raises two questions. One question is why there is such a small set of different prices (currently three in Massachusetts) that vary with time, not the level of use of the phone system.[16] A second question is why there are so few other examples of similar pricing. Presumably, the telephone companies find small advantage in additional price tiers and some, presumably small, cost in additional tiers. Probably more important than either costs or theoretical elasticities of demand is the issue of communicating with customers. Changing the rules involves a significant cost of communication with customers, although the information would be bundled with monthly bills. Probably also important is the extent to which individual customers (as opposed to businesses) would bother keeping track of a more complicated schedule. Presumably this factor also leads to a simple time-of-day price, rather than a price that varied with the level of usage and needed to be communicated continuously. Thus, even in the setting of highly predictable variation in demand and an automatic price adjustment rule, the variation in prices is limited. In contrast with a competitive (or monopoly) model with costless price change, prices change far

---

[15] Thus, I do not explore the variation in the average price of groceries coming from the distribution of prices between supermarkets and convenience stores and the different hours that they are open. Also not examined is the pattern of average prices when individual prices are showing stickiness and jumps in response to ongoing change in parameters, as with general inflation. See, e.g., Caballero (1989), Caballero and Engel (1991, 1992), Calvo (1983), Caplin and Spulber (1987), Caplin and Leahy (1991).

[16] Electricité de France does make some use of state-dependent pricing for large users. This does involve a short delay between announcing a change in price and its taking effect.

less often than would be predicted by theory. Whether the variance of prices is larger or smaller than would occur with continuous price adjustment is unclear.

In a number of other settings, there are regular price variations. Some electric companies follow this procedure. One commonly finds hotels and restaurants that vary prices. Many taxis have late night surcharges. Some stores offer senior-citizen discounts only on midweek days. No doubt some more examples could be found with an extended search, but it is not likely to change the picture that such price variation is unusual. Convenience stores do not vary their prices as neighboring supermarkets are open or closed. Prices do not vary with the length of customer lines at checkout counters. Stores do not offer high-price and low-price checkout counters, with different length lines. Stores use sizable discounts available only on some goods, not small variations in all prices, which could be easily programmed into cash registers.[17]

There are a variety of reasons for this lack of variability. Some of the lack may reflect the transactions costs (menu or sticker costs) associated with having different prices. Some may depend on organization costs – the difficulty of decentralizing price setting in response to observation of circumstances that are changing. Some may relate to consumer reactions to varying prices. Price variation in response to demand variation (as opposed to cost variation) seems to offend some consumers (Kahneman, Knetsch, and Thaler (1986)). Thus a theory of pricing needs to include a theory of the grouping of (potential) transactions for which the same price will be quoted, as well as a theory of the choice of a particular price.

Naturally, these issues have been central to consideration of the effects of inflation. For a variety of reasons, even steady money creation is not neutral; but exploring this would take us away from the central focus of these lectures. So, I will just mention the articles collected in

---

[17] I suspect that the very long delays (both after proposal and after first adoption) in the spread of one-way toll collection on bridges and tunnels reflects some of the same thought processes that affect the use of time-of-day pricing.

Eytan Sheshinski and Yoram Weiss (1993) on costly price adjustment. Naturally, one can not think about inflation without a time dimension.

While I will not explore the theory of price adjustment, I will consider some further evidence on this subject. Before turning to data on actual prices, I begin with an interview study by Alan Blinder (1992). From April, 1990 to March, 1992, Blinder and a team of graduate students interviewed 200 randomly selected firms about their pricing behavior. The firms were all located in the northeast of the US to facilitate interviews. Disproportionately, they were large firms. Otherwise they were chosen to be representative of the private non-farm for-profit, unregulated economy, with sample selection probabilities proportional to value added. Firms were asked: How often do the prices of your most important products change in a typical year? Obviously, the answer would be sensitive to inflation rates, and to relative price changes as well. 10 percent of firms said less than once a year, 39 percent said once a year. Only 15 percent said more than once a month.

Firms were also asked about the lags in responding to shocks, with demand and cost shocks and increases and decreases all asked about. One of the four similar questions was: How much time normally elapses after a significant increase in demand before you raise your prices? The mean answer was close to three months, with a standard deviation somewhat larger than the mean. Like the distribution of the frequency of price change, this presumably reflects differences across industries.

Blinder explored a dozen different theories of price stickiness. Interviewees were given a brief, jargon-free description and asked how important the idea was for the speed of price adjustment. All of the theories found some firms claiming that they were moderately or very important. The most frequently described as important were waiting for other firms to go first, waiting for costs to rise, preferring to adjust delivery lags or other aspects of the "good," and tacitly stabilizing prices for customers. But all of the theories had some acceptance. While one may be justified in modeling a representative industry with just one source of stickiness, to me this suggests that one should explore whether one's findings are robust to the source of the stickiness.

I turn next to several studies that have examined patterns of prices in actual transactions. First, I want to talk about the work of Dennis Carlton (1986, 1989), who has analyzed the Stigler–Kindahl (1970) data. Stigler and Kindahl collected data mainly from buyers, typically firms in the *Fortune 500*. Much of the data were collected monthly, over the ten-year period from January 1, 1957 to December 31, 1966. Carlton was interested in how long a firm would continue purchasing a product at exactly the same price. He was also interested in examining the patterns of prices paid at the same time by different firms. Let me quote some of his summary of his findings:

> The degree of price rigidity in many industries is significant. It is not unusual in some industries for prices to individual buyers to remain unchanged for several years.

> Even for what appear to be homogeneous commodities, the correlation of price changes across buyers is low.

> The level of industry concentration is strongly correlated with rigid prices. The more concentrated the industry, the longer is the average spell of price rigidity. (1986, p. 638)

In considering how alternative theories relate to these findings, Carlton has one section entitled the introduction of time, in which he examines some changes in the simple atemporal model that come from introducing time. In particular, he comments on intertemporal substitution in both demand and supply as elements that dampen price variation. Inventories and delivery lags are clearly part of such a story. So too may be allocation of limited supply to different buyers based on the supplier's relations to the buyers and the supplier's knowledge of the buyers' needs. Thus ongoing buyer–seller relationships matter, even when there is no contract. More generally, Carlton identifies price as just one of several variables relevant for the allocation of resources.

I wish to mention two more studies of infrequent price changes. Stephen Cecchetti (1986) reported the low frequency of changes in newsstand prices of magazines. Kenneth Koelin and Mark Rush (1990) have noted that some magazines reduced the number of non-advertising pages during the periods when they did not adjust nominal prices. Anil Kashyap (1990) examined prices in catalogs for mail order. Again the finding is one of infrequent price changes.

While I have not described the analysis of inflation using costly search theory,[18] I will take a moment to describe one recent empirical study. Roland Bénabou (1992b) compared the findings of theoretical models of costly search with inflation and costs of changing prices with US data on markups in the retail trade sector. Bénabou summarizes his findings as follows:

> Two clear conclusions emerge from this study. First, both expected and unexpected inflation have small but high[ly] significant negative effects on the markups of the U.S. retail sector. Secondly, neither inflation variability nor inflation uncertainty seem to matter. These results are broadly consistent with equilibrium (S,s) models where higher trend inflation, by causing more price dispersion, promotes search and thus intensifies competition ... Most importantly, they support the findings of many recent theoretical models that one of the most important welfare effects of inflation is its impact on market power. (1992, p. 574)

This conclusion is presumably sensitive to the fact that the range of inflation rates in the US is low, by international standards. Very high inflation rates undoubtedly introduce additional complications, particularly the difficulty in remembering relevant prices, that I suspect reverse some of the signs. Again, some of the theory calls for that result.

I have focused on prices of output in this chapter. Clearly I could have done a similar analysis of labor markets and wages, considering labor contracts (and the accompanying phenomenon of wage drift), considering

---

[18] See, e.g., Bénabou (1988, 1992a), Diamond (1991, 1993), Diamond and Felli (1990).

wages of steadily employed workers not covered by explicit contracts, and considering wages of day laborers.

2.4 Recessions

I have started these lectures by considering equilibrium in a single market. Using the standard market clearance assumption, we examined how uncertainty about costs and sunk costs of entry modify the way that fluctuations in demand affect prices and quantities. I then suggested that the usual market-clearing formulation was not an adequate representation of the relative speeds of response of firms and consumers and that this might require an alternative formulation of interaction in a single market – one that would be characterized by price dispersion over both time and space, as well as some infrequently changing prices. This is suggestive of issues that have been central in consideration of business cycles. Mention of business cycles raises the question of whether pricing works differently in good times and bad ones. Turning to Marshall again, he seemed to think so. He wrote:

> The immediate effect of the expectation of a low price is to throw many appliances for production out of work, and slacken the work of others; and if the producers had no fear of spoiling their markets, it would be worth their while to produce for a time for any price that covered the prime costs of production and rewarded them for their own trouble.

> But, as it is, they generally hold out for a higher price; each man fears to spoil his chance of getting a better price later on from his own customers; or, if he produces for a large and open market, he is more or less in fear of incurring the resentment of other producers, should he sell needlessly at a price that spoils the common market for all. (1948, p. 374)

And again:

> If trade is brisk all energies are strained to their utmost, overtime is worked, and then the limit to production is given by want of power rather than by want of will to go further or faster. But if trade is slack every producer has to

make up his mind how near to prime cost it is worth his while to take fresh orders. And here there is no definite law, the chief operative force is the fear of spoiling the market; and that acts in different ways and with different strengths on different individuals and different industrial groups. (1948, p. 498)

These quotations raise the question of whether we want to go further in reformulating behavior in single markets before addressing the economy as a whole. If we consider a sustained fall in demand in the standard Marshallian model, price falls further in the short run than in the long run. That is, in the short run, some firms continue to produce if they can cover their variable costs. In the long run, some of these firms exit the industry, reducing supply and raising the price. In other words, the short-run supply curve is steeper than the long-run supply curve. The quote from Marshall suggests that the short-run response to a fall in demand (that is expected to last awhile) may be an attempt to maintain prices, to avoid "spoiling the market." The quote implicitly distinguishes durable and non-durable goods markets in terms of the effect of a current cut in price on future demands. This may involve some of the issues raised above in discussion of intertemporal aspects of markups. Fear of spoiling the market may be related to the ability of firms to cover their financial commitments (as in Fisher (1933), Bernanke and Gertler (1990), Greenwald and Stiglitz (1993)) since it is not general deflation that concerns firms so much as a fall in the prices of what they sell, even if their costs are falling. A firm that will not survive a cut in price even if that raises sales has little reason to try that strategy, even if maintaining prices has little chance of success.[19] This dimension raises, in turn,

---

[19] As an example, consider the following atemporal model of a monopolist. Assume that profits of a firm are $P(p,z)$ where z is a random variable and the price, p, is set before the realization of z is known. Assume that P is increasing in z (where positive) and concave in p for any z. Assume that the firm maximizes the expected value of profits above the debt obligation, D. (This ignores implications for the future of failing to meet a debt obligation.) Then the objective function of the firm is $E\{\text{Max}[P(p,z) - D, 0]\}$. We are interested in the behavior of the optimal p as a function of D. If, in the certainty problem, the optimal p

the role of the level of investment (or overexpansion) during good times as an issue affecting the nature of recessions.

While there is obvious room for further analysis of single markets, I move on to considering models of an entire economy in my next lecture. The thrust of this lecture is to recognize both "space" and time as affecting equilibrium; models with a single homogeneous product traded in a locationless frictionless instantaneous market can not come to grips with the way trade actually happens. One way to view the relationship of these two lectures is to note the limits on acceptability of simple competitive models for micro when considering limits on acceptability of the same competitive framework for macro. This is part of the drive toward having a single way of looking at both subjects.

is monotonic in z, then, in the uncertainty problem, the optimal p is monotonic in D, with the same sign. Thus, if prices are higher when demand is higher, then a greater debt level results in higher prices.

As an alternative example, assume that the firm considers the future infinitely more important than the current moment (the reverse of the absence of a future in the paragraph above). Then, the objective function is to maximize the probability that $P(p,z)$ exceeds D. Thus, the objective function is Max $[G(z)|$ $P(p,z) \leqq D]$, where G is the distribution of z. Then, we have the same conclusion as above. One can construct examples that do not behave like these two.

APPENDIX A

This model extends the analysis in chapter 1 by having price-setting firms (rather than an auctioneer) and by having some non-searchers as well as the costless searchers of competitive theory. In each period, there is an upward-sloping supply curve, $S(k)$, of firms willing to enter if the expected present discounted value of profits exceeds their cost, k. If a potential firm does not enter it disappears, there is not an accumulation of potential entrants over time. Active firms face the exogenous probability a of terminating. The real discount rate is r. Changing the cost assumptions used in chapter 1, we now assume that every firm has a fixed cost of production, k', for any period of positive production. The firm can produce up to one unit of output. Before entering, the firm is uncertain as to its marginal costs. There are two possible costs, with $c_1 < c_2$. A potential entrant does not know whether it is a high-cost or a low-cost firm until after it has paid its entry cost, k. The entering firm learns instantly which type of firm it is. The fraction f of entrants are high cost.

There is a measure D of demanders, each of whom will purchase one unit if the price is no greater than u, with $u > c_2 + k'$. We assume that if everyone were a costless searcher (as in chapter 1) the market would clear with some of the high-cost firms voluntarily exiting. That is, we assume that the equilibrium price would be $c_2 + k'$. For this to be equilibrium, we need demand to lie in the interval of output produced by low-cost firms and by all firms:

$$(1-f)S[(1-f)(c_2-c_1)/(r+a)]/a < D,$$
$$D < S[(1-f)(c_2-c_1)/(r+a)]/a. \tag{1}$$

Appendix A

In contrast with this equilibrium, if everyone were a non-searcher, the equilibrium price would be u. We assume that the level of demand is such that, in this equilibrium, there would still be firms indifferent to exiting. Denoting the level of sales per high-cost firm by d, indifference to exiting implies:

$$d(u - c_2) = k'. \tag{2}$$

With all consumers being non-searchers, all firms have the same number of customers. Thus, this assumption on demand is:

$$(1 - f)S[(1 - f)d(c_2 - c_1)/(r + a)]/a < D,$$
$$D < S[(1 - f)d(c_2 - c_1)/(r + a)]/a. \tag{3}$$

Since d is no larger than capacity, 1, one side of each of the constraints in (1) and (3) serve as the bounds:

$$(1 - f)S[(1 - f)(c_2 - c_1)/(r + a)]/a < D,$$
$$D < S[(1 - f)d(c_2 - c_1)/(r + a)]/a. \tag{4}$$

We now assume that the fraction g of the demanders are non-searchers, while the fraction $(1 - g)$ are costless searchers. For g sufficiently small, we will continue to have the same single price equilibrium as occurs when everyone is a costless searcher. In such an equilibrium, all firms are producing at capacity (since otherwise a small price cut increases profits). This will be an equilibrium unless high-cost firms find it worthwhile to price at u instead. Such a firm will have demand equal to g (rather than 1) since only non-searchers will show up. Thus there is or is not such a single price equilibrium, as g is above or below a critical value of g, denoted g' given by the breakeven condition:

$$g'(u - c_2) = k'. \tag{5}$$

For more non-searchers than this level, we will not have a uniform price equilibrium at the price that occurs with all costless searchers.

We turn next to equilibrium where there are two prices. Let N_1 and N_2 be the numbers of low- and high-price firms and n the fraction of firms that charge the high price. The costless searchers all purchase from the low-price firms. The non-searchers are distributed evenly over all firms. That is, every firm has the same number of non-searchers. Since a low-price firm can attract all the costless searchers by an arbitrarily small cut in price, low-price firms all produce at capacity, 1. The high-price firms have sales denoted by d. Collectively the low-price firms attract all of the costless searchers and the fraction $(1 - n)$ of the non-searchers, and this total demand is equal to capacity, which is 1 per firm. The high-price firms satisfy the remaining demand:

$$D[1 - g + g(1 - n)] = N_1,$$
$$D[gn] = dN_2. \tag{6}$$

Taking ratios and solving for d, we have:

$$d = (1 - n)g/(1 - ng). \tag{7}$$

That is, the rules for allocating consumers to firms imply that d and n must satisfy (7).

All of the firms of one of the two cost levels will price the same, while the firms of the other cost level will be indifferent between the two pricing strategies. Since high-price firms attract only non-searchers, there is no reason for them to price below u. If high-cost firms are indifferent, then low-cost firms prefer a low price; if low-cost firms are indifferent, then high-cost firms prefer a high price.

For g a little above g', we have the case where there is a two-price equilibrium and high-cost firms are indifferent between the two prices, and indifferent as to whether they remain in production or not. Equal profitability for a high-cost firm with the two strategies, indifference to continued production and the customer allocation rule give us:

$$p - c_2 = d(u - c_2),$$
$$d(u - c_2) = k',$$
$$d = (1 - n)g/(1 - ng). \tag{8}$$

Solving for p and n, we have:

$$p = c_2 + k', \tag{9}$$

$$n = [g(u - c_2) - k']/[g(u - c_2 - k')]. \tag{10}$$

As g rises above g', we have equilibrium with n positive. We will continue to have such an equilibrium until there are no high-cost firms with a low price. This will occur at a level g'' where sales by all low-cost firms that were willing to enter just equals sales by low-price firms:

$$(1 - f)S[(1 - f)(c_2 - c_1)/(r + a)]/a = (1 - n)D \\ = D(1 - g'')k'/[g''(u - c_2 - k')]. \tag{11}$$

As g rises above g'' the price at low-price firms will rise, with no firms indifferent between the two strategies. Thus the number of low-price firms equals the number of low-cost firms and the number of high-price firms is the number of high-cost firms that do not exit, a number that preserves indifference to exiting. Combining the zero profit condition for high-cost firms and the consumer allocation equation, we have:

$$\begin{aligned} d &= (1 - n)g/(1 - ng), \\ d(u - c_2) &= k'. \end{aligned} \tag{12}$$

Thus (10) continues to hold. The price at the low-price firms will be at a level to induce enough entry to meet demand:

$$(1 - f)S[(1 - f)(p - c_1 - k')/(r + a)]/a = (1 - n)D \\ = D(1 - g)k'/[g(u - c_2 - k')]. \tag{13}$$

When g is high enough, low-cost firms will be indifferent between the two pricing strategies. In this case equilibrium becomes:

$$\begin{aligned} p - c_1 &= d(u - c_1), \\ d(u - c_2) &= k', \\ d &= (1 - n)g/(1 - ng). \end{aligned} \tag{14}$$

Thus, n satisfies (10) and p satisfies:

$$p = c_1 + k'(u - c_1)/(u - c_2). \tag{15}$$

This equilibrium occurs above a level of g, denoted g''', where supply equals demand at the price that has low-cost firms indifferent between pricing strategies:

$$(1 - f)S[(1 - f)k'(c_2 - c_1)/((u - c_2)(r + a))]/a = (1 - n)D$$
$$= D(1 - g''')k'/[g'''(u - c_2 - k')]. \quad (16)$$

Note the asymmetry that there is a single price equilibrium for values of g near 0, but a two price equilibrium for values of g near 1.

It is interesting to ask the question raised by Haltiwanger and Waldman (1991) of whether the costless searchers or the non-searchers are "more important" for the determination of equilibrium. A natural way to answer this question is to compare the average purchase price in the equilibria described above with the average of the two prices in the two equilibria if everyone were a costless searcher and if everyone were a non-searcher. Denoting this baseline average price by p_b, we have:

$$p_b = gu + (1 - g)(c_2 + k'). \quad (17)$$

Denote the average purchase price in equilibrium by p_a. If there are two prices, the fraction of the population paying the high price, u, is the fraction of non-searchers times the fraction of high-price stores, ng. Thus, we have:

For $g < g'$ $\quad p_a = c_2 + k';$
for $g' < g < g''$ $\quad p_a = ngu + (1 - ng)(c_2 + k');$
for $g'' < g < g'''$ $\quad p_a = ngu + (1 - ng)p;$ $\quad (18)$
for $g''' < g$ $\quad p_a = ngu + (1 - ng)(c_1 + k'(u - c_1)/(u - c_2)),$

where n is given by (10) and p varies with g as given by (13). There are two effects in the comparison of these two average prices. The presence of some costless searchers implies that some non-searchers find low-price firms, thus the weight on the price u tends to be lower in the actual equilibrium. On the other hand, the presence of non-searchers raises the price for costless searchers in some of the equilibria. The former effect is obviously more important in the bottom two regions. I conjecture that it is more important in the latter two as well.

Summing up, we see that a few non-searchers has no effect on equilibrium. More non-searchers imply some high-price firms and so some non-searchers paying a higher price. As the fraction of non-searchers increases, more and more of them pay the high price, but costless searchers are still unaffected. When the mass of non-searchers is large enough, costless searchers are affected too in that the price in low-price firms increases. Further increases in the fraction of non-searchers has no further effects on costless searchers, but continues to increase the fraction of non-searchers paying the higher price. The use of only two marginal costs, rather than a continuum, is responsible for some of this pattern.

APPENDIX B

This appendix presents the basic equations for the Butters model and then extends them to include non-searchers. In the model, the allocation of ads to customers can be thought of as generated by an urn-ball process, where customers are urns and ads are balls. Then the distribution of ads per customer is the Poisson approximation to the binomial distribution. Think of this as a model of the behavior of the post office.

Normalize the population of customers to be one. Denote the number of ads with price less than or equal to p by $A(p)$. Then, the probability of an ad with price p landing in an urn that has received no lower price quote is $\exp(-A(p))$. Thus the expected profit from an ad at price p (that is below the reservation price of customers, u) is $(p-c)\exp(-A(p))-b$, where c is the cost of producing the good for sale and b is the cost of sending an ad. The zero profit condition then gives the equilibrium distribution of advertised prices.

$$\exp[-A(p)] = b/(p-c) \text{ for } b+c \leqq p \leqq u. \qquad (1)$$

Now assume that the fraction n of customers are non-searchers. Of $A(u)$ ads sent, $nA(u)$ of them end up with non-searchers. Since the fraction $\exp(-A(u))$ of customers receive no ad, there are sales to $n(1-\exp[-A(u)])$ non-searchers. Thus the probability of a sale for an ad that goes to a non-searcher is $(1-\exp[-A(u)])/A(u)$. The fraction $(1-n)$ of ads go to searchers. Searchers select the lowest price ad, generating the same conditional probability of a sale as above. Thus the expected profit of an ad priced at p is $(p-c)\{n(1-\exp[-A(u)])/A(u) + (1-n)\exp[-A(p)]\}-b$. From the zero profit condition, the equilibrium number of ads with prices less than or equal to p, is now given by

$$\exp[-A(p)] = [b/(p-c) - n(1-\exp[-A(u)])/A(u)]/(1-n), \qquad (2)$$

over the range of zero profits. The upper bound of prices is u, as before. The lower bound is now endogenous, given by the equation

$$(p-c)\{n(1-\exp[-A(u)])/A(u) + 1-n\} = b. \qquad (3)$$

Solving (2) for $p=u$, we see that $A(u)$ satisfies

$$(1-n)\exp[-A(u)] + n(1-\exp[-A(u)])/A(u) = b/(u-c). \qquad (4)$$

Implicitly differentiating, we see that $A(u)$ is increasing in n.

LECTURE 2

MODELING AN ECONOMY

CHAPTER 3

SHORT RUN AND LONG RUN

In the first lecture, I examined equilibrium in a single market. I examined the distinction between short run and long run in Marshallian analysis, proposing an explicit modeling of time in place of Marshall's implicit modeling with different atemporal models for different time frames. The lecture was made easier by the common core of modeling shared by so much of the writing on partial equilibrium. It does not much matter what textbook one picks up in looking for examples. It does not matter whether one uses introductory, intermediate or advanced texts. One can look to Marshall for a presentation that is a widely shared antecedent.

When considering models of an entire economy, the story is very different. To begin, there are two very different traditions of modeling an entire economy. Both micro- and macroeconomists engage in this activity. The Arrow–Debreu general equilibrium model looks very different from the Hicksian ISLM model. Within microeconomics, there is considerable uniformity. But, not within macroeconomics. Compare Robert Barro's (1990) intermediate text with that of N. Gregory Mankiw (1992) and one sees significant differences in the modeling techniques thought to be important. The legacy of Keynes is treated differently in the two. Graduate texts such as Olivier Jean Blanchard and Stanley Fischer (1989) or Thomas J. Sargent (1987) do not resemble undergraduate texts, or each other. Thus my task here is more difficult.[1]

In the first lecture, I tried to portray a rich picture of the

---

[1] To avoid even more complications, I will treat a closed economy despite its shrinking relevance.

modeling of individual markets, based on models that consider different expansion paths for different firms and price competition with incomplete information. From that discussion, I hope you have concluded that the fact that the resource allocation process is spread out in real time means that the simplest market-clearing models are inadequate for many purposes. Thus, in thinking about the entire economy, the focus should not be on why prices do not adjust "right" but on how resource allocation (with frictions) works.[2]

Before considering formal models, I want to ask how models of an entire economy should differ from models of a single industry. That is, if we had models of single industries with which we were comfortable, what would we need in addition to have comparably comfortable models of an entire economy? The answer should lie in feedbacks from industries in general to individual industries. One example of such a feedback is the determination of overall income as it affects demand. Similarly, if the aggregate money supply or the availability of credit play a central role in the determination of demand or supply for individual industries, then we have a variable that needs modeling beyond what is done at the industry level. Another example is the general price level, or rate of increase in the general price level, which will affect a number of decisions at the industry level. While this is obviously important, I will focus on income levels, not inflation. This choice is a reflection of my level of study of different issues, with inflation on my agenda for future work.

Models of an industry take prices in other markets and incomes as given. Models of an economy consider all

---

[2] Robert Gordon (1981) has written that "there is no widely accepted explanation of the failure of markets to clear." In this article Gordon proposes the complexity of economic interactions (input–output relations) as the source of coordination failure. But it is the nature of the question that I want to underline. The question is based on a premise that one needs an explanation for why a theory that clearly does not fit the facts does not fit the facts. In the absence of such an explanation, other theories are suspect. This is a curious methodology, but one that appears to be widely shared.

prices at once and consider determination of the command over purchasing power along with the determination of prices. Micro and macro theories diverge in that the former focuses on determination of the vector of prices, while the latter focuses on the role of command over purchasing power, sometimes treating prices as parameters, not endogenous variables.[3]

3.1 Modeling equilibrium

It is unlikely that anyone would have noticed, but in the first lecture I avoided the word "dynamic." Instead, I contrasted explicit-time and atemporal models, implicitly making a case for both of them, one for theoretical analysis, the other for exposition and applications. This is in contrast with the way that the term "dynamic" is often used. As Paul Samuelson has written: "We damn another man's theory by terming it static and advertise our own by calling it dynamic" (1947, p. 311). Fritz Machlup has put this more colorfully:

> For more than twenty years I have been telling my students that one of the widespread uses of "Statics" and "Dynamics" was to distinguish a writer's own work from that of his opponents against whom he tried to argue. Typically, "Statics" was what those benighted opponents have been writing; "Dynamics" was one's own, vastly superior theory. (1991, p. 24)

On the use of the word "dynamic," Frank Hahn has written:

> It is difficult to think of words other than perhaps "struggle" which are more of an incitement to idle chatter than is the word "dynamic."

[3] The focus on purchasing power in this lecture results in the omission of the topic of "missing markets," a topic that also requires a model of an entire economy to properly analyze, and one that is important for understanding the efficiency properties of equilibrium. For analyses of the inefficiency of competitive allocations with missing markets, see Diamond (1967), Drèze (1974), Hart (1975), Geanakoplos and Polemarchakis (1986), and Geanakoplos, Magill, Quinzii, and Drèze (1990). For a discussion of some implications of missing markets which incorporates explicit time and repeated shocks, see Dixit and Rob (1991).

... to claim your theory to be dynamic often allows you to
get away with murder. (1984, p. 52)

Since the last thing I would want is to be accused of idle
chatter by Professor Hahn, I will continue avoiding this
term.

In any event, my vocabulary is different since my
purpose is different. In arguing for modeling in explicit
time, I do not mean that every aspect of resource allocation
needs to be explicitly modeled in time. That would yield a
structure too complicated to analyze. Rather, I am calling
for modeling part of the process explicitly, with awareness
of the time structure of the rest. I want to begin by
considering a somewhat different, but not altogether
different view. In his Yrjo Jahnsson Lectures, *The Theory
of Unemployment Reconsidered*, published in 1977,
Edmond Malinvaud has written about macroeconomic
analyses:

> In most cases the analysis is not "dynamic" in the sense
> that it would consider a process of adjustment; it is in fact
> plain equilibrium analysis, but operating with a specific
> concept of equilibrium.
>
> The true methodological question is to know whether some
> properly chosen equilibrium concept leads to a more effi-
> cient way of thinking about involuntary unemployment
> than an alternative formalization would do. If one objects to
> thinking with equilibria, one must use a dynamic formula-
> tion in which the relevant variables will simultaneously
> move according to some properly defined rules.
>
> We then quickly realize that a correct dynamic model
> cannot be simple. ...
>
> To rely on a general equilibrium formalization is to accept a
> short-cut, i.e. the consideration of only those equilibrium
> states that would result from dynamic adjustments. ... The
> result of the analysis then depends only on the definition
> chosen for equilibrium and not on the precise specification
> of the dynamic process that is supposed to lead towards
> this equilibrium. ... one feels that the direct consideration
> of equilibria permits a quicker grasp of the main questions
> than would the study of the dynamic adjustments.

> The type of consistency that is assumed to exist between individual decisions is specific to each equilibrium theory. For the study of unemployment it can only be a short-run consistency, which will be quite different from the long-run consistency that one will want to consider when studying for instance industrial structures. (1977, p. 5–7)

I have indicated that I do not disagree that an atemporal model can be instructive. My point is that the process of selection of the "right" atemporal model involves thinking about the resource allocation process over time, and that *some* of that thinking may be done better in an explicit model.

Malinvaud's remarks on the role of the definition of equilibrium are a good contrast to the natural tendency to take models too literally, a tendency that can get in the way of using them appropriately. In contrast with Malinvaud's approach, let me describe a brief exploration I made in the *New Palgrave*. There is no listing for sticky prices. Look up market clearing and you are directed to monetary disequilibrium and market clearing, an interesting entry written by Herschel Grossman. Let me quote:

> An explanation for the effect of monetary policy on real activity also must satisfy criteria of logical consistency ... the assumptions about economic behavior used to account for the relation between money and real activity should be consistent with the assumptions used to explain resource allocation and income distribution. ... The most unattractive aspect of monetary-disequilibrium theory is that, as yet, its proponents (who include most macroeconomists) have been unable to reconcile it with the postulate of maximization and the corollary that perceived gains from trade are exhausted.
>
> A frequent claim is that the existence of coordination problems reconciles monetary disequilibrium with the postulates of maximization. Various authors argue that, even with producers behaving as rational maximizers, perception and coordination of the wage and price adjustments necessary to clear markets in the face of unanticipated monetary disturbances takes time ... but it seems irrelevant for the analysis of monetary disequilibrium because the values of monetary aggregates are public infor-

mation. In contrast to truly private information, the monetary aggregates are not information that the price system has to convey.

This implication is that disturbances to monetary aggregates affect real aggregates only to the extent that currently available information does not permit agents to infer current monetary aggregates accurately. ... (1987, vol. 3, p. 504)

Implicit in Grossman's presentation is an atemporal model where the collection and publication of aggregate statistics is simultaneous with transactions for which the level of demand is influenced by the same factors that generate the aggregate statistics.[4] A real time process would not have this simultaneity, so an atemporal model of the same phenomena need not have this "type of consistency ... between individual decisions."

More generally, modeling of equilibrium must consider the speeds at which events happen.[5] The simplest models have everything happening at one speed. Explicit-time models generally have an atemporal part. That is, the models have two speeds, but with one of them infinitely faster than the other. One example is Bénabou's (1989)

---

[4] Also implicit is a model of individual behavior that has a degree of understanding of the economy and a level of actions based on this understanding that seem to me unrealistic. For an alternative view of individual reactions to monetary phenomena, see Shafir et al. (1992).

[5] In moving from consideration of a single industry to consideration of an entire economy, I am skipping over consideration of multiple markets. It is interesting to note that Hicks felt that the distinction between short and long runs was not useful when considering multiple markets. In Value and Capital, he wrote: "First of all, there are some parts of his [Marshall's] model that we shall hardly find it worth our while to retain. The rigid tripartite division (Temporary Equilibrium on the first 'Day', Short Period, and Long Period) is the most important of these. These categories are suitable enough for Marshall's isolated market, but they hardly fit the analysis of the whole system. There is scarcely any period of time so short that it can give us temporary equilibrium (in Marshall's sense) for all commodities...There is scarcely any nameable period of time so long that the supply of all commodities can be 'fully adjusted' within it" (1946, p. 122).

I do not plan to spend any time discussing the timing aspects of interactions in multiple markets. The slow transmission of price changes through the large array of linked markets has indeed received some attention. See, e.g., Gordon (1981) and Blanchard (1983).

treatment of search, where search is infinitely faster than price adjustment. Another example is the use of Poisson processes for trade (e.g., Diamond (1982)) where negotiation and conclusion of a trade is infinitely faster than the process of meeting potential trading partners. The problem with having two different speeds with a finite ratio is the complexity in the interactions. The dimensionality of individual decisions and of model accounting both go up greatly. So models typically have a temporal part and an atemporal part. Yet the need for handling more models with multiple speeds persists. As Marshall wrote: "as a rule, no two influences move at equal pace" (1948, p. 368).

3.2 Arrow–Debreu model

One model of an entire economy is the familiar general equilibrium model, the Arrow–Debreu model.[6] This model has a rich time structure of the production and delivery of goods and labor. But the structure of the coordination of trade is totally atemporal. All trading takes place at one moment in time, with perfect coordination. Moreover, this theory is primarily a theory of relative prices, in the sense of the focus of attention. For example, consider the text by Kenneth Arrow and Frank Hahn (1971). After a historical introduction, they begin their presentation with a section entitled "The Problem":

> Our main concern will be the description of situations in which the desired actions of economic agents are all mutually compatible and can all be carried out simultaneously, and for which we can prove that for the various economies discussed, there exists a set of prices that will cause agents to make mutually compatible decisions. (p. 16)

The Arrow–Debreu model does have incomes in it. The levels of income that are needed for determining demand are the present discounted values of the proceeds from the

---

[6] See, e.g., Debreu (1959) or Arrow and Hahn (1971). For examples of the use of the Arrow–Debreu model, see Lucas and Prescott (1974), Kydland and Prescott (1982), Prescott (1986, 1991).

sale of endowments (including labor) over the rest of time plus the pure profits of firms owned by the consumers (plus lump-sum redistributions, if any). The profits of firms, like other sources of income, can be expressed solely as functions of prices. Moreover, the planned spending of income is simultaneous with the clearing of markets – there is no time structure to the budget constraint, no uncertainty with missing markets that would be modeled as multiple budget constraints.[7]

Firms do not have budget constraints in the Arrow–Debreu model. Yet it is clear that access to financing does affect the behavior of firms. But I shall focus on households and not consider models that relate the business cycle to the availability of funds to firms.[8]

An alternative route into describing an entire economy is to focus on income and trading, giving short shrift to relative prices. This is the approach of macroeconomists, sometimes working with a single aggregate consumption good. This difference in emphases has been stated very succinctly by Mankiw:

> Micro is about relative prices. Macro gives income a central place. (1992, p. 16)

A central concern of this lecture is the modeling of the command over purchasing power, while continuing attention to the modeling of price setting.[9] By using the ISLM model, not the Arrow–Debreu model, as the central atemporal model, I am accepting concern with the modeling of purchasing power as central for macro. This view is

[7] See, for example, Diamond and Yaari (1972).

[8] There is an important role for purchasing power in supply, and the related investment demand. For analyses of this linkage, see Fisher (1933), Bernanke (1981, 1983), Gertler (1988), Bernanke and Gertler (1990), Greenwald and Stiglitz (1993).

[9] The balance between these two issues in recent macro research has been heavily on the side of price setting. For example, despite the quotation from Mankiw's text, the collection of readings, *New Keynesian Economics*, edited by Mankiw and Romer (1991) is primarily about prices, not income. The section headings are "Costly Price Adjustment," "The Staggering of Wages and Prices," "Imperfect Competition," "Coordination Failures," "The Labor Market," "The Credit Market," and "The Goods Market." Only two of these seven sections are about the command over purchasing power.

similar to the view taken by Martin Hellwig (1993). He concludes that paper with:

> Since the ascent of Walrasian general-equilibrium analysis in macro- as well as microeconomics, the investigation of income feedback processes has gone out of fashion. I suspect that this reflects the weakness of the theory rather than the irrelevance of the problem. A naive observation of the evolution leading into the current recession would seem to suggest that – at least in the short run – income feedback processes are at the centre of macroeconomic dynamics. The fact that such processes cannot be analyzed within a framework that focuses attention on "equilibria" should not lead us to conclude that therefore they are unimportant. [p. 47, footnote omitted]

Thus, I will be giving the ISLM model the same place in thinking about entire economies as the Marshallian model in thinking about an industry.

Before leaving the Arrow–Debreu model, I want to make a few observations. The Arrow–Debreu model is atemporal in the way in which the future impinges on the present. This has been described by Arrow and Hahn (1971) as:

> The economy we have been considering is an abstract one in many respects, but perhaps the most serious departure from what we expect the world to be "really like" is the supposition that there are enough futures markets to produce "coherence" not only in the markets for current goods, but also in the markets for future goods. This hypothesis "telescopes" the future into the present, and although this occurs at least partially in certain markets, we know that it does not take place either universally or over the distant future. (p. 33)[10]

One line of research that builds on the Arrow–Debreu model without having all trading at once is the temporary equilibrium literature (Grandmont (1988)). This literature

[10] On the relationship between the present and the future, Hicks wrote: "It is fundamentally important to realize that the decisions of entrepreneurs to buy and sell (and to some extent also the similar decisions of private persons) nearly always form part of a system of decisions which is not bounded by the present, but has some reference to future events. The current activities of a firm are part of a plan, which includes not only the decision to make immediate purchases and

models trading as repeated competitive trading; at each period we have the same Walrasian structure as in the Arrow–Debreu model, with trade only for current commodities and claims for future income. Use of this model is limited by the considerable difficulty in tracking an economy interestingly through a sequence of these periods. In addition, the temporary equilibrium literature can be modified to fit more closely with Keynesian considerations (Grandmont and Laroque (1976), Benassy (1982)).

Expectations are central to temporary equilibrium modeling and are obviously important for the workings of the economy. The response of expectations to experience is therefore extremely important for following an economy over time. This issue has been the focus of extensive research; for example, see the work of Grandmont (1983, 1992). However, in these lectures I am focusing on other aspects of the time dimension and treat expectations in the simplest possible way. Thus this analysis is a complement to, not a substitute for that line of research.

3.3 Causing a recession

In the next chapter, I turn to formal models. But first, I want to present some empirical studies in order to give an image of the facts about entire economies which should be kept in mind when considering theoretical models. The first study is a description of a well-known empirical fact – that central banks can cause recessions. The second line of research is less well known. It is the pattern of prices and quantities over the course of a year. It seems to me that the quest is for a model that can speak to both of these.

Everyone knows that a central bank can cause a recession whenever it wants. I want to begin by summarizing a study by Christina Romer and David Romer (1989) that calculates how long and how deep a recession caused by the Fed lasts. Of course this is a reflection of both the

sales, but also the intention to make sales (at any rate, and usually purchases as well) in the more or less distant future" (1946, p. 123).

pattern of contractionary policy followed by the Fed and the lags in the effects on the economy, a combination that they do not try to disentangle.

Romer and Romer began by combing the records of both the Board of Governors of the Federal Reserve System and its Federal Open Market Committee. The purpose was to identify occasions when the Federal Reserve concluded that it would attempt to lower the rate of inflation, despite the output consequences that would follow.[11] They identified six such occasions in the period from World War II to 1980 – October 1947, September 1955, December 1968, April 1974, August 1978, and October 1979. This implies that six of the eight postwar US recessions up to the date analyzed were preceded by a decision by the Federal Reserve to reduce inflation. Then they created thirty-seven dummy variables to represent the month of such a decision, or a month up to three years after such a decision. They used these dummy variables in an autoregression explaining the change in the log of the monthly total industrial production series compiled by the Federal Reserve Board.[12]

Specifically, the rate of growth of industrial production was regressed on monthly dummies, twenty-four lagged values of itself and these thirty-seven dummies for Federal Reserve Board intent to lower inflation. A simple summary of their findings is conveyed by examining the impulse response function. That is, given the coefficients from their regression, they examined what would happen to industrial production as a result of the effect of the dummies and of the feedback of industrial production on later industrial production. By cumulating these effects, one has an estimate of the impact of Federal Reserve policy on output as well as standard deviation bands (see figure 3.1) (Romer and Romer (1989), figure 4, p. 155).

---

[11] Central banks do not cause recessions just for the fun of it. Thus the determinants of the rate of inflation must play a major role in a complete analysis of an economy. Since I have not engaged in an extensive study of inflation, I will say little about this subject. But the omission is not a reflection on the importance of the subject.

[12] They also examined the unemployment rate.

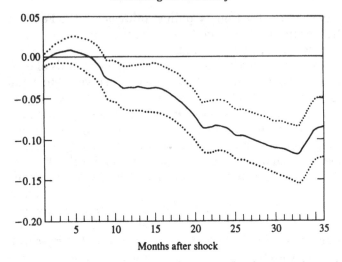

Figure 3.1 Impulse response function for basic industrial product regression

Romer and Romer find that for the first several months after such a decision, there is little effect on industrial production. Production then falls sizably. The maximum decline occurs about thirty-three months after the Fed's decision and represents industrial production that is approximately 12 percent lower than it would otherwise have been. Keep in mind that industrial production is about twice as volatile as GNP. Presumably both the size and the lag depend on the way that the Federal Reserve phases in its policies as well as the lags in the workings of Federal Reserve actions on the economy.[13]

Extending the regression and the dynamic calculation

[13] The paper also reports some robustness checks, particularly to the presence of supply shocks. Dropping the 1974 and 1979 events from the data set (as the two prime oil shock events) reduces the maximum impact of industrial production from 12 percent to 10 percent, but otherwise leaves the results basically the same. Alternatively, adding a supply shock variable to the regression barely alters the results. The supply shock variable used is the current value and first thirty-six lags of the monthly percentage change in the ratio of a weighted average of producer price indexes for crude foodstuffs and feedstuffs, crude fuel, and crude petroleum to the producer price index for finished products.

another twenty-four months, there is still a 7 percent drop in industrial production five years after the Federal Reserve began its action. This length of time suggests that monetary policy has long-lasting effects not simply summarized in the standard concept of a recession.

In work done since publication of this paper, the authors have added the most recent recession to their data set and find basically similar results.

Thus, the image coming from this study is that the response of the economy to the attempt to reduce inflation is a process considerably spread out in real time. I think of this image as a complement to that portrayed in the Davis–Haltiwanger study of employment flows described in Lecture 1. I turn now to the seasonal patterns of prices and output.

3.4 Seasonal patterns

At much smaller scales than that of business cycles, economies fluctuate in their behavior in the course of a day, in the course of a week, and in the course of a year.[14] The week is a social construction, sometimes backed by legislation, that results in different behavior of different sectors of the economy during the week and over the weekend. I do not know of aggregate data broken down in this way although we saw a little about retail price differences over the week. However well the organization of the economy adapts to social timing contrivances, there appear to be real effects. For example, there appear to be real effects on the timing of behavior from having all of China in a single time zone.

The seasonal pattern over the year is at a scale sufficiently large that we think of the category of seasonal jobs (as opposed to varying levels of staffing over the week).[15] Moreover, there are two aspects of the seasonal pattern.

---

[14] For a discussion of fluctuations at different time scales, see Hall (1991).

[15] In my summary of Romer and Romer, I mentioned that monthly dummies were used in their autoregressions. The importance of these dummies is an indicator of the level of variation I am considering here.

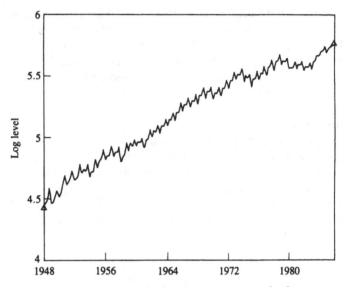

Figure 3.2   Log level of real output, quarterly data,
1948:1–1985:4

One is related to weather, with significant differences between the northern and southern hemispheres. The other is related to social organization, particularly the role of Christmas in the OECD data that have been gathered and analyzed.

To present this information, I want to quote from the lecture given by Jeffrey Miron at the Sixth World Congress of the Econometric Society, summarizing work he has done with Robert Barsky, Joseph Beaulieu, and Jeffrey MacKie-Mason. First, let me show you a graph of quarterly GNP for the US for 1948 through 1985 (see figure 3.2) (Barsky and Miron (1989), figure 1). You can see the importance of quarterly swings relative to business cycle effects from the magnitudes in the graph. The greater importance of seasonals can also be seen in the graph of quarterly growth rates (see figure 3.3) (Barsky and Miron (1989), figure 2). Seasonal patterns are not only large, but show some of the same characteristics as business cycle patterns.

To document the importance and patterns of seasonal

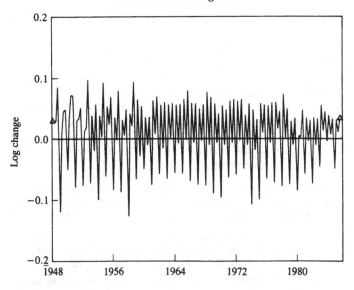

Short run and long run

Figure 3.3   Log growth rate of real output, quarterly data,
1948:2–1985:4

variation, the research by Miron and his coauthors begins
by regressing the first difference of the log of a variable,
such as GDP, on seasonal dummies, which may be quarterly or monthly, depending on data availability. Then, the
standard deviation of the fitted values of the regression
coefficients on the dummies is compared with the standard deviation of the residuals. These then represent
seasonal and non-seasonal variation. This is done for
many variables and many countries. Miron (1994) reports
his findings as follows:

> most macroeconomic quantity series are highly seasonal.
> For example, seasonal dummies usually explain more than
> 70% of the variation in the growth rate of real GDP. In
> contrast, the seasonal dummies explain only a small frac-
> tion of the variation in the growth rate of the price level.

> The pattern of seasonal variation is strikingly similar all
> over the globe. The most significant feature of this world
> wide seasonal cycle is a large decline in output from its
> peak in the fourth quarter to its trough in the first quarter. In

a typical country GDP rises by 4–5% from the third quarter to the fourth and then falls by 5–10% from the fourth quarter to the first. This pattern is consistent across most of the countries considered, including those in the Southern Hemisphere. The natural explanation is an increase in demand for goods associated with Christmas ... There are several countries in the sample that do not celebrate Christmas per se, but each celebrates a fourth quarter gift-giving holiday. The first quarter trough in GDP is present across hemispheres, challenging the view that it reflects the effects of winter weather.

Total output peaks in the fourth quarter. ... Manufacturing activity, however, peaks in most countries early in the fourth quarter or even at the end of the third quarter.

A second dramatic feature ... is a slowdown in industrial production at some point in the summer months. This slowdown is evident in all Northern Hemisphere countries... Two aspects of this pattern suggest that it does not result mainly from variation in the weather. First the slowdown is highly concentrated in a single month in most cases ... Second, the timing of the slowdown (July or August) differs across countries that have identical timing in the peaks and troughs of their weather patterns.

Australia displays a slowdown in manufacturing during the Southern Hemisphere summer.

[An] important stylized fact about business cycles is the widely documented comovement of nominal money and real output. ... this stylized fact characterizes the seasonal cycle as well as the business cycle.

[A] key business cycle fact is the cyclical behavior of labor productivity. ... The results show that the changes in labor input over the seasons are generally associated with more than one for one changes in output.

The description above refers to individual seasonal patterns. Miron has also examined the relative seasonal patterns across countries and across industries. His central findings appear in figures 3.4 and 3.5 (Miron (1994), figures 1 and 2):

Each figure shows the standard deviation of the seasonal component of industrial production for an industry or a

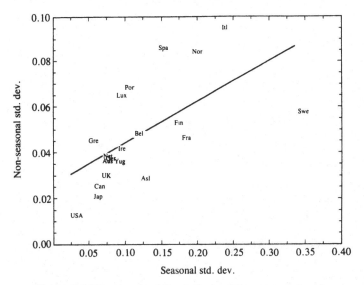

Short run and long run

Figure 3.4 The standard deviations of the seasonal and
non-seasonal components of industrial production for
different countries

country on the horizontal axis and the standard deviation
of the nonseasonal component on the vertical axis. The key
observation is that the two quantities are strongly, posi-
tively correlated. ... this result holds for a broad range of
aggregate variables.

Miron concludes that the seasonal and business cycles
result from the same propagation mechanism. In all of the
time frames, the firms and households that make production decisions, pricing decisions, and purchase decisions are the same firms and households. The different
time frames are relevant for the behavior of the different
variables. So too is the uncertainty of the length of time of
phases.

Combining my earlier summary of Romer and Romer
and these results, we have to recognize that economies are
subjected to different kinds of demand disturbances,
unless we are prepared to accept the unlikely answer to the

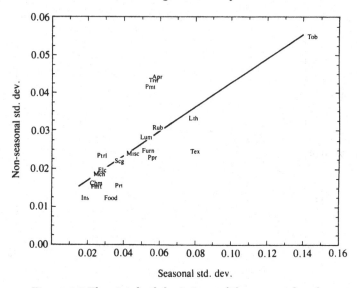

Figure 3.5 The standard deviations of the seasonal and non-seasonal components of industrial production for different US industries

question in the title of a recent working paper[16] – Does the Fed Cause Christmas? In addition, there are disturbances associated with supply, coming, for example, from oil price changes and from the desire to have a vacation in August. It seems to me that micro and macro should meet in facing these facts.

3.5 Medium run

Before moving on to a discussion of theoretical models, it seems appropriate to briefly consider time scales longer than those of a business cycle. Olivier Blanchard and Lawrence Katz (1992) have examined the time shape of the difference between state and national unemployment rates in the US. Using VARs, they describe the typical pattern of

---

[16] I remember seeing such a title, but could not locate the paper to cite it properly.

response of a deviation of employment growth. They find that it takes five to seven years after a shock for the unemployment and labor force participation rates to return to their long-run levels. During this period (and longer), wages are also below trend. As Barry McCormick (1991) points out, regional patterns are quite different in different countries. In particular, in the UK, regional unemployment is considerably more persistent.

Olivier Blanchard and Lawrence Summers (1986) have looked at persistence of unemployment rates at the national level. The presence of extended periods, on the order of decades, of high and low unemployment rates are present in the US and UK data that they present as an introduction to their analysis of hysteresis of unemployment.

A similar picture emerges in terms of the Beveridge curve, the relationship between unemployment and vacancies. Over a business cycle, an economy moves along such a curve as unemployment and vacancies move in opposite directions. However, Beveridge curves themselves also appear to shift. That is the entire Beveridge curve at some times seems to be outside the Beveridge curve at others (see, e.g., Blanchard and Diamond (1989)).

It appears that the natural rate is itself affected by actual unemployment rates. For example, consider the treatment of unemployment in Mankiw's text. In the labor market he distinguishes the natural rate of unemployment from cyclic unemployment. He cites the level of sectoral shifts among industries or regions, unemployment insurance, minimum wage laws, unions and collective bargaining, and efficiency wages in the chapter on long-run unemployment. When he comes to measure the natural rate of unemployment, he uses the centered two decade average of actual unemployment, without explanation. He does have a discussion of "hysteresis," of reasons that a recession might raise the natural rate, but this is brief and receives no formal presentation.

It is interesting to contrast this with the output market. In Mankiw's text, implicitly, the "natural rate of unemployment" in the output market is zero. Of course, firms do hold inventories and inventories do fluctuate relative to sales. I have not checked, but I would be surprised if the average level of the inventory–sales ratio moved up and down for an extended period in response to the lagged level of aggregate demand.

While I will not address modeling beyond the time scale of a business cycle, the presence of these slower moving adjustments should be kept in mind.

I have long believed that developing a good model of frictional unemployment was a critical step in getting better models of cyclic unemployment. The data on job creation and job destruction in chapter 1 give one indication of the magnitude of the frictions in the economy. The data on seasonality give another perspective on this magnitude. A modern economy has an enormous task of adapting to changes and the need for changes. The problems caused by business cycles, and the difficulty in responding to them, come, in part, from the presence of this vast sea of change, larger in fact than the typical business cycle effects that (rightly) play such a central role in policy. The juxtaposition of these two analyses was to force consideration of the issue of whether one wanted to think about these two phenomena in exactly the same way, or whether there were critical differences that should be kept in mind when engaged in model building.

CHAPTER 4

MONEY, INCOME, AND CREDIT

In thinking about an entire economy, one of the critical research choices is how to relate the way that one models entire economies to the way that one models individual markets. One approach has each of these research activities proceeding independently of the other, with industry studies focusing on individual firm and household data and economy studies focusing on aggregate data. An alternative approach attempts to develop a consistent way of addressing both classes of issues. I have been part of this second group, working in what has been called the micro foundations of macro.[1] This lecture will continue in this mode.

There are three broad categories of approaches for modeling purchasing power. Some models focus on income (with or without a role for interest rates), some models focus on money (again, with or without a role for interest rates), and some models focus on credit.[2] It is hard to use a model that addresses all three sources at once.

I will proceed by considering the Hicksian ISLM model, and then turning to explicit-time models. In the first lecture, I contrasted a single explicit-time model with atemporal models to illustrate the importance of paying more attention to time. For this lecture, I use several explicit-time models, each with some of the properties we would like such a model to have.

---

[1] As a "school," the micro-foundations literature starts with the Phelps (1970) volume. It has also been suggested that what we really need is a macro foundation for micro.

[2] Some barter models have inventories playing the role of either income or money; for example, Diamond (1982).

4.1 Short run and long run

As in the first lecture, I want to start with the contrast between the short run and the long run. Malinvaud draws this distinction as follows:

> If quick adjustments of prices occur with many agricultural products and raw materials, nothing similar prevails with the prices of manufactured goods, the prices of services and wage rates. In the long run goods, services or types of labour that are more and more in demand, and cannot be more and more supplied at constant real costs, will undoubtedly tend to experience an upward shift in their prices in comparison with those that are in the opposite situation; but such a shift will occur mainly as a result of differences in the relative magnitude of price rises when they take place, and this does not usually happen at very frequent intervals. (1977, p. 9)

As one would expect, this contrast between short and long run is stated sharply in some textbooks. For example, Mankiw writes:

> To build a model of short-run fluctuations, we must first decide how that model will differ from the long-run classical model. ... Most macroeconomists believe that the crucial difference between the short run and the long run is the behavior of prices. *In the long run, prices are flexible and therefore can respond to changes in supply or demand. In the short run, however, many prices are "stuck" at some predetermined level.* Because prices behave differently in the short run than in the long run, economic policies have different effects over different time horizons. (1992, p. 215)

There is a contrast between the usual statements of the short-run–long-run distinction in micro and in macro. In micro, the structure of interactions is the same in the short and long runs, only the range of individual actions is different. In macro the distinction is usually stated in terms of interactions – in the short run, prices do not clear markets.[3] This contrast goes away if we use a price-setting

[3] See, e.g., Mankiw: *"Over short periods of time, prices are sticky, the aggregate supply curve is flat, and changes in aggregate demand affect the output of the economy. Over long periods of time, prices are*

rather than a quantity-setting long-run model. Then the short- and long-run macro models would differ in the extent to which firms change prices, closely paralleling the micro distinction. With a price-setting approach, both short- and long-run models need theories of the determination of transactions given the setting of prices. Presumably the sizes of the response of demanders to different prices are different in the two runs, just as short- and long-run demand elasticities are different in Marshallian theory.

Macro differs from micro in its attention to purchasing power as well as in its approach to prices. The Marshallian model did not treat income differently in the long and short runs. In contrast, long- and short-run macro models differ in the role assigned to purchasing power. The long-run macro model is the neoclassical growth model. Fluctuations in unemployment are simply ignored, output is equal to supply in these models. Thus prices clear markets. Moreover, lifetime considerations determine demand. In contrast, short-run models have a distinction between notional demand and effective demand. The latter reflects both activities in other markets and liquidity considerations. For example, in the sticky price literature (Barro and Grossman (1976), Malinvaud (1977), Benassy (1982)) sticky (or preset) prices in the labor market are at the center of analysis of the output market (and vice versa). By and large, however, the macro literature focuses on the behavior of prices as the major difference between short and long runs. For example, Hall and Taylor (1991) write: "Price adjustment takes the economy from a position described by the short-run model to one described by the long-run growth model" (p. 124). Adjustments in access to purchasing power also seem important in this transition. Credit arrangements often need rearrangement; physical assets often need to be bought or sold before other adjustments can be made. These processes take time. To move this discussion to formal modeling, the natural starting place is the familiar ISLM model.

flexible, the aggregate supply curve is vertical, and changes in aggregate demand affect only the price level." (1992 p. 224).

4.2 ISLM

I start with the simplest macro model. We all know the basic Keynesian cross model of equilibrium. Consumption is written as a function of income. Investment and government spending are taken as given. The equilibrium level of output satisfies the equality of income and output where consumption is equal to the demanded value:

$$Y = C(Y) + I + G. \tag{1}$$

Consider the time structure inherent in this atemporal model. We see that all prices are given (or irrelevant), consumers are able to consume the amount that they want given their levels of income. Similarly, investment and government expenditure are at their desired levels. While this is an incomplete theory, lacking a number of pieces, the time structure is straightforward. So too is the direction of research suggested by this starting place – enrich the theory of the determinants of consumption, investment, and government spending; look elsewhere for a theory of the determination of the (fixed) level of prices.

Although the focus of these lectures is the time structure of interactions, it is worth noting that people who use these models enrich the theories of consumption and investment demands by treating the time dimension of individual choice more carefully.[4] The intertemporal dimension of lifetime utility maximization, and therefore the distinction between income changes with different expected durations, is an important part of consumer demand theory. Similarly, the costs of adjusting, or reversing, investment decisions makes the myopic view of investment demand less attractive than more forward-looking ones.[5]

It is natural to compare this model with the atemporal

---

[4] In addition, lags between government decisions to increase expenditures and actual increases in expenditures have been studied in detail. Similarly, the role of taxes as built-in stabilizers reflect lags in legislated tax changes. For a model of built-in stabilizers, see Diamond (1994).

[5] For an essay emphasizing the importance of expectations, particularly rational expectations, see King (1993).

Marshallian model of the first lecture. Just as one can build expectations into the supply curve of the Marshallian model, one can build expectations into the consumption and investment functions here. The issue is not what can be done, but what can be learned from complementary research approaches.

The textbooks also contain the complementary theory of aggregate demand based on money. While stated as a demand for money, when we add the assumption that money demand equals money supply and that both prices and money supply are exogenous, it becomes a theory of the determination of income. The simplest version is the Cambridge equation that money demand is proportional to income. Stated in real terms, we have:

$$M/P = kY. \tag{2}$$

The time structure is inherently the same as that in the first model. Micro foundations, such as the Baumol–Tobin inventory control theory of the demand for money, are based on a more detailed study of the time structure of individual transactions.

Since the models in equations (1) and (2) have basically similar inherent time structures, it is easy for the textbooks to put them together. Of course, two equations, each determining the same variable is not a workable approach. So we assume that, unlike other prices, interest rates adjust quickly, and add the interest rate as an endogenous variable. This leads us to the ISLM model of Hicks, a theory with predetermined prices, but endogenously determined income and interest rates.

Putting interest rates into all functional forms,[6] we then have:

$$Y = C(Y,i) + I(Y,i) + G,$$
$$M/P = L(Y,i). \tag{3}$$

---

[6] Following standard practice, I do not make government expenditures a function of interest rates, although such a relationship is likely to follow from political economy models of the determination of expenditures, particularly state and local expenditures. I do not bother distinguishing between real and nominal interest rates.

This model has a single interest rate. For applications of this model, it is often important to recognize the full term structure of interest rates, since different parts of the model are sensitive to different rates. Considering the term structure, one naturally considers expectations running different distances into the future. For example, discussions on the short-run impact of Clinton's proposed deficit reduction package hinged critically on the term structure effects and expectations in the bond market.

Purchasing plans and the finance constraint

In the atemporal Marshallian model, the length of time of a period is judged by the time it takes for a range of actions to play out, whether it is the adjustment of output by a firm, or entry and exit. We need to ask about the length of time implicit in this atemporal model of an entire economy. In particular, with both price adjustment and purchasing power access varying with the time frame, the issue of an appropriate atemporal model is complex. In presentations of the ISLM model, the time dimension of variables is not usually specified. In the Keynesian cross model, (1), what is the length of time over which the flow of income is measured for the model to apply? It surely is not relating consumption on a daily basis to income on the same basis. Nor weekly. Perhaps quarterly; at least that is the time frame for GDP data commonly examined with this model. But this raises the question of whether anticipated quarterly income has the same impact on planned quarterly spending as deviations of income from anticipations has on actual spending. One might also be concerned about different responses (in both planning and realization) in different quarters, reflecting the seasonality discussed above. Another question is whether the income variable that appears in the model is accrued income or realized income or (in a complex interaction) both? This contrast comes into focus when thinking about inventories.

Similarly, in equation (2), what is the time period over which income is accrued to have the relevant variable for the demand for money. Presumably this depends on the

concept of money that one is employing. Money for transactions is presumably related to a shorter time span of
income than a larger set of liquid assets (also denominated
in nominal units). Perhaps, since planned transactions
relate to a longer income frame, so too does transactions
demand for money.

Interestingly Hicks does not discuss the length of a
period in his 1937 classic presenting the ISLM model.[7]
Nor do the textbooks, at least the ones I consulted.[8] If a
model of the economy differs from a model of an industry
by considering the command over purchasing power, then
we need to ask what atemporal models will capture the
way command over purchasing power plays out in real
time. Presumably atemporal models looking at different
time frames (seasonal as opposed to business cycle
lengths) will be constructed differently. A model for
thinking about December will be different from a model
for thinking about a recession. The time dimension of the
purchasing power side of a model needs to reflect both
spending plans and actual transactions. In making spending plans, budget constraints are relevant. These constraints involve accumulated assets and debts and expectations about income and expenditure needs extending
some distance into the future.[9] In actually acquiring
goods, a quid pro quo is required, whether it is money or
the promise inherent in credit from the supplier or in

[7] The only reference I could find to period length was the following.
"Thus I assume that I am dealing with a short period in which the
quantity of physical equipment of all kinds available can be taken as
fixed" (1937, p. 148). This reference to technology does not relate to the
structure of market interactions.

[8] Some texts make no mention of the length of a period. Blanchard and
Fischer (1989) write: "How short is the short run? To that question,
there is no easy answer. It is clear that using the fixed price IS–LM
model to study medium- or long-run effects of policy or that maintaining the assumption of fixed prices while allowing for dynamics of
capital accumulation, for example, is at best inappropriate. In that case
one must embed the IS–LM in a model that allows for an explicit
treatment of aggregate supply and of price and wage adjustment"
(p. 531).

[9] On a longer scale, the difference between the optimal growth model
and the overlapping generations model is a difference in the treatment
of budget constraints (Ramsey (1928), Diamond (1965)).

credit from a third source.[10] Money can be acquired from previous sales of goods and services, from sales of assets, or from activating access to credit.

All of these planning and spending activities have time dimensions. Unfortunately for modeling convenience, the evolution of budget constraints and the evolution of financing constraints happen at different speeds.[11] While it is common to assume that interest rates adjust instantly, this is a reflection of the workings of organized asset markets and does not describe the pairwise credit extension that is important for both consumption expenditures and investment. Thus, it is convenient either to focus on budget constraints and purchasing plans or to focus on financing constraints and transactions.[12] This is a tension between the two approaches behind equations (1) and (2). Putting them together, as in (3), there is the difficulty with the tendency of each of them to move at different speeds. Moreover, the relative importance of the two pieces will vary with economic conditions. For example, hyperinflation changes the importance of the time frame of purchasing power feedback, as both payment periods and indexing periods get shorter. Put differently, the velocity of money is endogenous, with velocity depending on both bank and non-bank behavior. In other words, while the framework of the ISLM model is valuable in organizing thinking about the short run of an economy, we would not expect great stability in the values of some of the parameters. One of the purposes of micro foundations is to develop a theory of the parameters that are not stable in aggregative analyses.

---

[10] That is, a detailed model needs a purchasing-power-in-advance constraint. These can come in various forms. The cash-in-advance constraint was introduced by Clower (1967). For a discussion of the relationship between individual and aggregate "finance constraints" see Kohn (1981).

[11] A sense of the difficulty in combining these elements can be obtained by examining models that have tried to do this. See, for example, Grossman and Weiss (1983), Rotemberg (1983), Romer (1987).

[12] The Arrow–Debreu model has budget constraints based on the entire future, with a structure that relies on the assumption that the organization of trade happens instantaneously (and before time really happens). There is no finance constraint.

For contrast with the atemporal ISLM model, I will review the way in which the command over purchasing power plays out in some explicit-time models.[13] I start with a model where lags in spending convert earlier income flows into later purchasing power. Next is a barter model where produced inventories are the command over purchasing power. Then I consider credit as a supplementary source of purchasing power. After considering these models without a role for a central bank, I turn to models where the supply of money from the central bank plays a major role in determining command over purchasing power. In each of the models, there are simplifications of the determination of spending plans that allow a focus on financing. Price adjustment also plays out over real time. Most of the models considered have perfectly flexible prices; although two of them have an information structure that gives perfectly rigid prices relative to the time frame of the determination of the command over purchasing power.

Prices

Before turning to purchasing power, I want to review the issue of price determination. Prices play no role in the model portrayed in (3). Thus one could replay the model in successive periods, adding an equation for the predetermined prices at the start of each period as a function of outcomes in the previous period. This is not the way that Mankiw, among others, proceeds. Instead, he views the model in (3) as a model of aggregate demand and adds an equation for aggregate supply, turning the price level into another endogenous variable.[14] In particular, he presents the equation that output equals a constant plus a multiple

---

[13] For a comparison of the ISLM model with an explicit-time model, see Kohn (1983).

[14] In using a deterministic equation, without a random term, I am not only leaving out the "noise" that is part of the focus of Hall (1991), but also supply shocks. Central for the concern with purchasing power is the question of whose income (if anyone's) is enhanced by a supply shock. This issue increases in importance once one uses an open economy model for analysis.

of the difference between the price level and the expected price level:

$$Y = \bar{Y} + a\,(P - P^e). \tag{4}$$

Mankiw presents four different "micro" theories that all reach this equation – sticky wages, worker misperceptions, imperfect information, and sticky prices. Now, one needs an equation for price expectations. Moving into first differences, Mankiw introduces the expectations augmented Phillips curve and, for simplicity, static expectations about the inflation level.

In contrast with this short-run model, Mankiw's long-run model has a vertical supply curve – the level of output is independent of the price level, or, in first difference terms, the level of output is independent of the rate of inflation.

In chapter 2, we examined some evidence on price adjustments. While some prices are adjusted frequently, many are not. In low inflation times, the average price level moves slowly and many prices do not change over a period of several months. Thus the assumption of fixed prices in equations (1) to (3) could apply to a moderately wide range of (short) lengths of time. However, in the fourth equation, we have a significant role for errors in forecasting the price level. If prices move slowly, then we would not expect significant errors in aggregate price forecasting over a short period of time. Thus there is a basic tension between the desire for a relatively short time period in order to have fixed prices and a relatively long period in order to have significant price expectation errors.

This tension comes primarily from thinking of price expectation errors as a causal variable for individual quantity decisions and would be lessened if we approached the ISLM model in terms of price setting by firms. Then, equation (4) becomes a relationship between pricing behavior and the level of sales. P^e is then the level of prices that would be set if sales were at the level $\bar{Y}$. For the logic of price setting, we would want to identify a price and sales pair from which we measured deviations. The full employment level of output is not a natural candidate as a benchmark for individual price setters. To explore this issue one would want an explicit-time model of price-setting behavior in the presence of sunk costs and some fixed contracts. While I have not tried to build such a model, I suspect that we would want to identify continuation of the trend inflation rate with a continuation of the level of output, adjusted for "recent" shocks and normal growth. This would give different benchmark levels of output ($\bar{Y}$) in different settings, with short recessions and extended ones having different benchmarks. This would parallel the way that the history of entry and exit affected the choice of the short-run model in chapter 1. The equation coming from such analysis would recognize that prices are not fully set (or predetermined) but adjust somewhat "within the period." This is similar to the way one would approach the phenomenon of "wage drift" in a model of centralized bargaining over the wage contract.

From this perspective, the substantial literature on over-lapping contracts and overlapping periods of unchanged prices represents an explicit-time modeling of the role of historic factors in the current responsiveness of the economy. This includes the (S,s) pricing literature cited above (for example, Caplin and Leahy (1991), Caballero and Engel (1991, 1992)) and the older contract literature focused more on the labor market (Fischer (1977) and Taylor (1979)). This has a clear parallel with the use of explicit-time modeling of cost variation and cost uncertainty to illuminate the parameters of the atemporal short-run Marshallian model in chapter 1. In pursuing the Marshallian model in explicit time, I dropped the "representative firm" as an assumption that got in the way of analysis. The same need holds for many questions of macro. As James Tobin put it over twenty years ago:

> The myth of macroeconomics is that relations among aggregates are enlarged analogues of relations among corresponding variables for individual households, firms, industries, markets. The myth is a harmless and useful simplification in many contexts, but sometimes it misses the essence of the phenomenon. (1972, p. 9)

4.3 Inflation in a wartime economy

Explicit(discrete)-time modeling marked the work of Dennis Robertson (1926), and of the Stockholm School.[15] In keeping with the paucity of statements in theoretical work about the length of a period, Robertson (1959, p. 36) refers to "the formidable difficulties in the way of making precise the conception of a 'period.'"[16]

According to Björn Hansson (1982), the distinction between plans and actions is central to distinguishing the length of a period for the Stockholm School. In his algebraic discussion, Erik Lindahl (1939) has prices and purchase plans set at the start of a period and carried out during the period, leading to a (possible) revision of plans for the start of the next period. The length of a period is related to the length of time for which a plan is left unchanged, to be acted on. Lindahl recognizes that the lack of synchronization of the timing of plan revisions implies that it is a very short period when no one is revising plans. "But in order that the length of the period may not become too short to be plausible, we shall assume, not that all individual plans are kept entirely unchanged, but that the resulting sums (or averages) of the individual values only show negligible change during the period considered. In this way our reasoning may in general be applied to such relatively short periods as days" (p. 125). Erik Lundberg (1937) devotes considerable attention to the difficulty of defining a period for sequence analyses. He makes it clear that his "day" is not a chronological day; so while there is discussion of alternative lags, there is not an empirical statement about applicability.

In my view, continuous-time modeling of this process is conceptually cleaner, but has considerable mathematical difficulties, especially when different factors have differ-

---

[15] For expositions of various lengths, see Hansson (1982, 1987, 1991).

[16] Although it has only a slight connection with the modeling of time, I want to quote Robertson (1959, p. 144). "Perhaps we should all agree that, if only we knew how to get it, what would really be most convenient is a population which is always growing but never getting any bigger."

ent lag structures and different speeds of response.[17] In contrast, discrete-time modeling has the complementary difficulty of trying to determine the length of a period and the allowed implicit structure of interactions "within the period." Arrow and Hahn (1971) have a somewhat different view. In a section entitled "Stock and Flow Equilibrium," they write:

> Connected with the distinction we have been discussing is the device of "period analysis." This can be helpful in overcoming some of the conceptual problems raised by continuous time, but it also can be misleading. For instance, Swedish authors at one time found it helpful to define the length of the period by the time interval over which prices could be taken as fixed. Starting with given prices at the beginning of the period, a flow equilibrium over the period, then, would involve stock disequilibrium at the end of the period unless the economy was in full equilibrium. They then traced the economy from period to period by using certain rules for changing prices. In an economy with many agents, however, it seems unnatural to suppose that they all not only adjust their preferred action at discrete intervals, but they do so at the same moment. If that is not so, then such adjustments will be taking place more or less continuously. To this must be added the fact that period analysis leads to a formulation in terms of "difference equations," which are capable of producing motions for the system that are not possible if the formulation is in terms of differential equations, so that what started as an aid to visualization may finish by being pretty misleading. (p. 50)

The simultaneous revisions inherent in discrete-time periods are unrealistic for many settings (although calendar time does result in some coordination). Part of the attraction of the recent analyses where individual actions are staggered and spread out in real time is the ability to make sense of different timing of actions by different agents. The issue of staggering as opposed to coordinated timing in contracts and price setting is clearly important.

---

[17] Differential equations with deviating arguments, also called mixed difference-differential equations, are difficult to analyze. Thus the

I turn now to the first of the explicit-time models I will discuss, a model of Tjalling Koopmans that appeared in 1942 as a continuous-time mathematical analysis of the determinants of the rate of inflation in a wartime economy, with analysis that was meant to be a first-order approximation only when inflation rates were low.[18] This is a market-clearing model, one that determines the equilibrium level of inflation in order to have market clearance.

The starting place of the analysis is the assumption that with output fixed (a condition relaxed later in the article), war expenditures would cause real demand to exceed real supply if the previous level of aggregate consumption is maintained. The equilibrium level of inflation is then the rate that will bring about equality between demand and supply given the lags in receipt and spending of income.[19]

The heart of the model is the division of income between labor and non-labor incomes, with the assumption that the former is spent immediately and the latter with a lag.[20] To begin, nominal wages are assumed to adjust continuously so that real wages are constant. In the introductory case, the equilibrium rate of inflation is equal (to first order) to the share of output demanded by the government for the war (net of decreased investment because of controls), divided by the share of private income not going to labor times the lag in spending such income. This lag is the lag from when it is earned until it is spent, not just the lag from when it is received until it is spent. Thus the delay in the payment of dividends figures significantly in selecting an appropriate number for calculated examples.

The paper analyzes seven additional cases, considering a considerable list of complications. The first complication

appeal of assumptions that collapse such structures into ordinary differential equations.

[18] There is a large literature employing lags in spending. I selected this one for its straightforward presentation and for the example of a microeconomist thinking about an entire economy in this way.

[19] The model considers spending on consumption – there is savings, but no investment in the model.

[20] Given institutional developments over the last fifty years, the interest paid on money not yet available or not yet spent (e.g., dividends not yet paid) would now be part of the analysis.

is a marginal propensity to consume out of non-labor income less than one. The second is a lag in the adjustment of wages to prices, which redistributes from labor income (with a propensity to consume of one and no lag) to non-labor income with a lower propensity to consume and a lag. Koopmans considers several different formulations of the wage adjustment lag, distinguishing between cases of synchronized adjustments and adjustments evenly spaced out in time. He considers the effect of taxes, distinguishing the differential rates of tax on labor and non-labor incomes and including the loss in real tax revenue from delayed collection under inflation. He distinguishes income from fixed long-term interest rates and rent payments on the one hand from entrepreneurial income, insofar as there are different propensities to consume out of these incomes. He considers the possibility of increased employment and output, marking the important distinction between competition (with no marginal markups) and cases where there are markups, so that increased output implies increased non-labor income (which is the only income subject to lags). And he considers speculative demand – the effect of inflation of increasing demands either because of the desire to accumulate stocks for the future or because of increased measured income from inflation. All in all it is a very rich analysis.

In some textbooks, the circular flow of goods and income plays a central role in the introductory material. Koopmans' model sets the atemporal circular flow diagram in explicit (continuous) time. There are several directions one could pursue to generalize the simplest explicit-time circular flow model. This paper pursued the variation in average lag according to the type of income. The directions not pursued include endogenizing the lag as part of a decision process, disaggregating aggregate flows of different types of income into individual receipts of income, having a capital market, and so a role for balances in the process of being spent, and individual production and pricing decisions. The focus was on income, not money, as a determinant of spending. The models discussed next address some of these issues; however, in order to preserve tractability, they drop the diversity in types of income flows that is the centerpiece of Koopmans' analysis.

4.4 Costly search

Several simplifications contribute to the tractability of Koopmans' analysis. One is that output is given (at the full employment level, or as a simple function of the real wage). A second is that inflation is just at the level that clears the output market. To move away from these two assumptions, one needs a theory of price setting, and a response of output to aggregate demand given this price-setting structure. I turn now to some of my own writings on search theory (Diamond (1984b), Diamond and Fudenberg (1989)). These are models where, as in the Koopmans model, there are no commitments to price that interfere with transactions. However, by focusing on pairwise trade rather than idealized-market trade, an endogenous level of production is made dependent on the level of income. The different models I and others have worked on explore different ways of describing the access to purchasing power.

To purchase a good, one must have goods to barter, or money to pay, or a creditor willing to cover the transaction. The creditor may be the supplier of the good or a separate supplier of credit. Access to these sources of purchasing power are themselves dependent on past experience in transactions, particularly sales. The distribution of purchasing power in the economy is also affected by production decisions. For example, the decision to hire workers to produce goods for sale puts purchasing power in the hands of workers. My intent when I started developing a general equilibrium costly search model was to trace the circular flow in a model simple enough to keep track of it, yet with some economic decisions that were sensitive to the way the flow worked.

The easiest case to work with is a barter economy, although that has the difficulty that the same variable is serving as demand and supply. The logic of the model will be familiar to some readers; its structure is straightforward. Production is carried out in order to have goods to trade. Trade takes place involving only the goods that have been produced. The critical assumption is that trade is quicker when more goods are available for trade; the transactions technology has increasing returns to scale. This is a proxy for the experience of suppliers who have significant fixed costs so that a drop in sales represents a serious drop in profitability.[21] This feedback loop from high production to high profitability of production and so to high production could be modeled in a variety of different ways. All of them have the property that where there are relevant marginal decisions to be made, the equilibrium has too little production since there is an externality created by additional production. Since it is assumed that all mutually advantageous barter transactions are carried out, there are no "sticky prices" in this model.

For some combinations of parameters, there are multiple steady-state equilibria. This opens up an array of different types of non-steady-state equilibria. The critical links are that expectations of profitability drive the production decision (as they do) and that the assumption of rational expectations does not pin down the model since there are multiple rational expectations equilibria. Thus one can have convergence to good and bad steady states. One can have cycles. If one complicated the analysis to have differential equations of higher dimension, one could have all sorts of possibilities. The approach opens up many possibilities, perhaps too many. So one needs to pin down this process in some way, so that history will play more of a role and "animal spirits" will have less free rein. The model contains nothing resembling an accelerator, which could be used to pin down some of the swings in the level of demand.

It is clear from the structure of this analysis that the assumption of barter is convenient, it is not necessary for the results. The convenience comes from the ability to

---

[21] My belief is that there are sharply different short- and long-run returns to scale in many production and trading activities.

describe the economic position of an agent by a 0–1 scalar, the stock of inventory. The aggregate position of the economy is then describable as a scalar, the fraction of the population with (unit) inventories. The incentives in the economy are summarized, again, by a scalar, the shadow price of a unit of inventory, modeled as the difference in the dynamic program values of two economic positions – with and without inventory. A great deal of the simplicity comes from the assumption of an *ex ante* representative agent, although there are two positions these agents could be in at any time. It is easy to add some complications to the model, as long as they preserve the simplicity of the accounting of the positions of different agents and as long as incentives can be described in one or a few terms.

To see some of the complications that can arise with greater realism, consider allowing any (integer) level of inventories. This requires tracking the distribution of inventory holdings in the hands of different agents. This accounting is doable; by itself, it adds a little to the difficulty of solving the equations of the model. The real complications come from the shadow prices for additional production for inventory and from the prices for trade. With different levels of inventory, there are different incentives to produce for inventory since the greater the stock of inventory, the later an additional unit of inventory will be used in trade. With discounting in utility, we then have a decreasing willingness to produce as a function of the inventory level. This wealth effect may or may not be realistic, but the point here is the increased complication of analysis.

The logic of bargaining over price is also more difficult in an economy where there are different positions traders can be in. Trade is one-for-one when all potential traders have a single unit of the good and all potential traders have the same preferences (as a result of intertemporal additivity in lifetime utility, implying no effects from the lag since there was last consumption). However, when agents are in different economic positions, then bargaining theory suggests that negotiated prices will vary with their positions. We are interested in such price determination, but it greatly complicates the accounting of inventories. Either inventory levels become continuous (rather than being the integers) or some trick must be used to have a smoothly varying price and still have unit inventories.[22] The difficulty in solving these models while extending them interestingly has limited the accumulation of results.[23]

The bottom line, as in the Koopmans study, was to have an explicit-time structure that can inform simple atemporal models. While the basic idea can be captured in an atemporal model, the research process seemed to go best with an explicit-time structure. Again, as with the Koopmans study, the model was restricted to only some of the elements that matter for the behavior of an entire economy.

Credit

In the Koopmans model, previous income was the source of purchasing power. Whatever the role of lending and borrowing and interest rates, it was subsumed in the pattern of lags. In the costly search barter model, previous production was the source of purchasing power; there was no role for lending and borrowing and interest rates. Trade credit provided by the seller has been incorporated in an extension of this model (Diamond (1990)). In this extension, the arrangement of credit (when it is available) is instantaneous relative to the search and production processes. That is, in some meetings, one agent has a unit of good in inventory, while the other does not. The one with a unit of inventory considers delivering the good in exchange for a promise to deliver goods in the future. The

---

[22] One such trick is to allow varying quantities from a single opportunity (with or without a sunk investment). This has been used by Shi (1992) and Trejos and Wright (1993). An alternative trick is to allow trade of lotteries, with one agent handing over goods for sure, while the other hands over goods with a probability less than one. This probability then serves the same role as a price. This trick has been used in Diamond (1990).

[23] I have also pursued an alternative approach to modeling the circular flow, making use of two types of agent (worker and capitalist) and a continuous level of inventories or money holdings (Diamond and Yellin (1985, 1987, 1990)).

model explores the limits on when such credit is provided (based on credibility of future payment) and the determination of the interest rate when it is provided.

This credit model allows exploration of the feedback loop that greater general availability of credit increases the willingness of individuals to extend credit. That is, individuals are more willing to extend credit when they have easier access to credit themselves, or their borrowers have easier access to substitute credit. The paper shows that this feedback loop can result in multiple equilibria. Since trade possibilities affect the incentive to produce for inventories, the financial and real parts of this economy are jointly determined.

By combining barter and credit transactions into a single structure, this model avoided the problems of modeling access to intermediated credit. Borrowing comes in many forms. New loans and accessing existing credit lines move at different speeds. Renewal and refusal to renew existing loans move at a speed related to existing contract durations. Since the behavior of intermediated credit is an important part of the behavior of economies, modeling these patterns in a way that is consistent with the rest of the model is an obvious, although difficult route to pursue. There is a sizable literature on the micro foundations of intermediated credit that has recently been surveyed by Mark Gertler (1988). It would be interesting to explore some of these models in alternative explicit-time settings.

I will not describe this literature beyond considering one recent paper by Nobuhiro Kiyotaki and John Moore (1993). In this paper, collateral is necessary for borrowing to purchase assets.[24] Thus the value of existing assets plays a critical role in the ability to borrow, and so in the allocation of resources. The model uses discrete time, with simultaneous provision of collateralized credit and market determination of the price of existing assets, which are part of this collateral. This market is followed by a production

---

[24] For evidence that declining property values limit refinancing of mortgages after interest rates decline, see Caplin, Freeman, and Tracy (1993). For an overview of evidence on the importance of credit availability, see Gertler and Hubbard (1988).

process with uncertainty at the individual level. Kiyotaki and Moore follow the model over time, showing a tendency for small shocks to be magnified and for damped cycles. The time dimension of this model comes from the fact that incentive compatibility issues make collateral important; future incomes can not serve as an adequate basis for borrowing. This means that a rapidly adjusting price in the asset market has large effects on borrowing ability. This model does not recognize the range of different liquidities of different assets and the need to sell some assets (particularly in the housing market) as a convenient way to finance asset purchases.[25] Modeling of liquidity would naturally focus on the time dimension of the transactions process. The model developed by Kiyotaki and Moore is designed to focus on one major issue and as it is is considerably complicated. It would be good to have additional models exploring the interaction of liquidity, borrowing constraints, and resource allocation.

4.5 Cash in advance

An alternative way to model the time structure of organizing purchasing power is to focus on money, requiring people to convert alternative forms of wealth (or access to credit) into money before using the money to purchase. There is a sizable literature using discrete time models to analyze the effects of such a constraint. I will not attempt an overview of this literature, but just describe a few papers to review the time structure.[26]

Typically, these models have a discrete time structure. Purchases within a period can only be made with money acquired at the start of a period. The simplest version of this model has a given velocity of money, since money is

---

[25] For a partial equilibrium study of the housing market where the sale of houses (on a search market) follows the purchase of an alternative place to live, with the lags affecting prices, see Wheaton (1990).

[26] One source for papers of this type is the volume edited by Kohn and Tsiang (1988). For recent analyses including some discussion of empirical findings, see Christiano and Eichenbaum (1992a and b).

used once in each period.[27] There are a variety of ways of endogenizing velocity. One recent example is by Robert Lucas (1990). In this model, a family divides its available funds between a purchaser of commodities and a transactor in the bond market. This endogenous division of money gives an endogenous velocity. The commodity side of this model has competitive markets with prices that clear these markets. Such an assumption is not needed to be able to solve the model. Assuming that prices are set in advance (and so making an assumption on the time structure of actions and information) significantly changes the model, as we will see in a moment.

Sticky prices

I turn now to a pair of models that have prices that are set in advance of knowledge of the aggregate level of demand. One is by Lucas and Michael Woodford (1993), and the other by Woodford (1990) alone. Like Lucas (1990), these use discrete rather than continuous time and have money, not income, as the central player in determining effective demand on the time scale relevant for the stickiness of prices.

In chapter 2, we identified lots of reasons why firms are slow to change prices. And, we noted that there are generally many different prices at which homogeneous goods are available. There are many partial equilibrium models that can be built to yield price distributions. One route is to have costly price changing and goods that were priced at different times. A different route is to have multiple equally profitable strategies available to firms. Lucas and Woodford choose the latter and use the model in Prescott (1975), discussed in chapter 2. Aggregate demand is simply uncertain and firms must price their goods before knowing aggregate demand. Since consumers are assumed to successfully seek out the lowest available price, different prices imply different probabilities of sale.

---

[27] With money flowing from households to firms and back to households in one period, this might be considered using money twice.

The condition of equal expected profits for different prices gives the equilibrium distribution of prices.[28]

It is not surprising that with prices set before demand is known, there are unsold goods, which is the equivalent of unemployment. Interestingly, as discussed above, one does not need to have predetermined prices for this result. Slow revelation of information can yield the same result.

Lucas and Woodford place this atemporal model in an intertemporal discrete-time setting, with consumers receiving money at the start of each period, a random shock to aggregate monetary receipt, and firms learning about demand from observing sales, not from knowing the aggregate of money available. Thus they are combining a sequential-service constraint, a cash-in-advance constraint, and aggregate uncertainty about money supply. The Lucas–Woodford model is a stringing together of atemporal models with limited connection between periods. The connection between periods is kept limited by an assumption of insurance markets that place all consumers in the same position at the start of each period. The stringing together is needed for one aspect of the model, the evaluation of money carried forward in time which, in turn, is central for determining reservation prices.

Consumers all have the same reservation price for buying the good, a reservation price that depends on the monetary shock. Consumers might spend all of their money or might carry some forward to future periods. The firm does not observe this reservation price, although the firm knows the distribution of the common reservation price (determined by the distribution of monetary injections) when setting its pricing policy. Thus this is a model where prices are set in advance (of full knowledge of demand) in recognition of the uncertainties of demand. As the firm sells successive units of its inventory, it may stock

---

[28] In a continuous-time model, different strategies imply different average lengths of time of goods in inventory or different levels of sale relative to the fixed costs of having a batch of goods available for purchase. In a labor setting, it would be different expected durations of spells of unemployment.

out (if demand is high) or have units left (if there are fewer customers willing to buy than might have been). For optimal pricing with risk neutral firms, the expected revenue from each unit for sale must be the same.[29] But the expected revenue depends on the pricing behavior of other firms. Lucas and Woodford find a symmetric solution to this pricing game. The details of the equation need not concern us.

In this model (as in some others), the random policy of the monetary authority is the source of all economic difficulty. The Okun-gap-like shortfall of sales from potential sales comes from the random injections of money that are not observed until after sales are completed. However, as soon as one adds a real basis of uncertainty, then information problems continue and full efficiency can not be restored by a constant money supply policy. This situation has been analyzed by Woodford, who modified the model above by adding randomness in the aggregate number of consumers with positive utility from consumption. In Woodford, unlike Lucas and Woodford, different consumers face different prices and have different consumption levels. That is, Lucas and Woodford had all consumers making the same fractions of their purchases at the different prices in the market. In Woodford there is an efficiency issue in that consumers are risk averse relative to the prices they will face.

Continuing the cash-in-advance constraint, Woodford has consumers go to the monetary authority to borrow the money they will use to purchase during the period. The monetary authority is subject to the same sequential-service constraint in setting interest rates at which it will lend to consumers. Thus loans are being made without knowledge of the full extent of demand for the period. Woodford shows that the optimal monetary policy accommodates demand fluctuations, generating variations in money supply and thus in the level of sales. This accommodation provides insurance for consumers who

---

[29] This assumes non-storability of the good, as well as independence of demand from pricing in previous periods.

face the risk associated with different prices for different transactions. Woodford shows that the unique monetary policy that maximizes the *ex ante* expected utility of the representative individual involves no variation in the nominal interest rate in response to the aggregate demand variations.[30] That is, to keep money fixed would require very high interest rates on some consumers, and this risk is more costly than the forgone output with fluctuating demand.

Of course, this policy conclusion is dependent on the structure of a very special model. But let me note one of the virtues of this approach. We can do welfare analysis within the context of the model. That is, analysis of policy takes place in a model in which the sources of inefficiency are the pieces of the model. Of course, I do not mean that such policy implications should be taken literally, any more than I mean that such a model should be taken literally. Rather, I want to contrast this structure of analysis with a policy discussion built around the ISLM model. One must add to that model some tradeoff between inflation and output in order to consider the policy implications of the model. But the reasons for this tradeoff are not sufficiently important for the workings of the economy to be included in the model. One can proceed this way. But, I suspect interesting things can also be learned by trying to proceed in a more integrated fashion.

Let me elaborate on this point. Economists are familiar with the idea of an equity–efficiency tradeoff. Attempts to redistribute income lead to distortions in the economy. Thus one wants to strike a balance. One way to think coherently about such a balance is through a general equilibrium model that relates the market equilibrium to the types and level of redistribution. This is the approach that the optimal tax literature has taken (Diamond and Mirrlees (1971)).

Stabilization questions frequently have similar tradeoffs. Expenditure and tax changes may be desired for their

[30] As mentioned above, there is insurance to put all consumers in the same position at the start of the next period in order to simplify the intertemporal dimension of the model.

micro consequences and for their macro consequences. Monetary policy affects consumer borrowing and investment as well as inflation and unemployment. There is then a use for a unified model that can consider both micro and macro dimensions. For example, there was much political heat about the (very small) stimulation package that President Clinton proposed, with the Republicans objecting because of its contribution to the deficit. The level of public debt is relevant for resource allocation. The level of short-term stimulation is also relevant. It is not farfetched that the discussion of this issue can be improved by a modeling approach that attempts to include the most important ingredients of both types of resource allocation questions in a single tractable model.[31]

In the Lucas–Woodford model there is no multiplier-like feedback of sales on demand, no simultaneity in income determination and price adjustment. Development of these micro environments in a setting including such feedbacks seems to me to have potential for thinking about micro and macro simultaneously. In particular, one could then have a basis for judging the appropriate amount of stabilization, which will involve trading off different distortions.

Also missing in the model is any cost associated with expected inflation. It is the randomness in monetary policy that leads to unsold goods. A continuous-time model will tend to have effects from foreseen inflation as well.

4.6 Time frame

In chapter 3, we considered price and quantity fluctuations over the year as well as examining business cycles. How should models differ that relate to these different time frames? One obvious difference between them comes from predictability. While recessions may follow expansions with the same inevitability of night following day,

[31] For a more extensive discussion of this perspective, see Diamond (1994). For example, one can analyze the effects of higher marginal tax rates as larger built-in stabilizers as part of the calculations that also balance equity and efficiency.

Sunday following Saturday, and Christmas coming in December, the predictability of when the recession will come is clearly different. Second the lengths of the time frames themselves are different.

It seems to me that the differences in uncertainty about timing, while important, are not central to the needed modeling differences. The time frame itself seems central, representing different weights on different demand factors (that move at different speeds). First I will argue that the presence of considerable uncertainty at all times decreases the importance of the difference in uncertainty. Then I will consider the budgeting and spending opportunities and behaviors of people and how they vary over different time frames.

I will consider households, but there are similar issues for firms. Households have wealth, debts, and current and anticipated income flows. They have opportunities to borrow, to invest, and to spend on consumption. There are uncertainties associated with any plans for the future. The loss of a job is a risk that a sizable fraction of the population faces at all times, as suggested by consideration of the gross flows of workers, as discussed in chapter 1. A recession raises this risk. Uncertainty about when a recession will end seems considerably less important than the increase in risk per se. Losing a job may imply a period of unemployment (unless a new job is found between the announcement of the end of employment and the actual end of employment). The random length of time until a new job is found (and the quality of that job) are affected by the state of the business cycle. Again this seems more important than the issue of when a recession will end. If the typical duration of unemployment were considerably longer, then expected changes in job finding probabilities would loom larger in describing incentives and outcomes. Thus the timing of some investment decisions will be sensitive to predictions of the timing of turning points, and important in determining that timing.

Job beginnings and job endings have large seasonal components as well as cyclic ones. Obviously, this holds for seasonal jobs. I suspect that it also holds for non-seasonal jobs – permanent hirings and separations for jobs of indefinite length probably are concentrated when seasonal labor needs are at turning points.[32]

Similarly, the length of seasonal jobs seems relevant for demand implications, not the predictability of the timing of their end. I suspect the relationship between the seasonal pattern of earnings and the seasonal pattern of spending is different from the relationship between their cyclic counterparts. It would be interesting to examine whether countries that have the institution of a large Christmas (or December) bonus have larger Christmas effects in spending. Even if true, the feedback mechanism is likely to be different just because of timing. Actual spending for Christmas presents out of Christmas bonuses does not do much for employment in manufacturing that produced goods for inventory in September and October, although forecasts of their level do matter. In contrast, it may be the case that business cycle turning points are affected by actual spending as well as forecasted spending. Thus the multiplier process varies with the time frame being analyzed.

In addition to income flows, access to new credit (and continued access to current credit) also varies with the state of the business cycle. Having the Fed follow a policy of seasonal smoothing of interest rates probably makes nineteenth- and twentieth-century seasonal patterns look different (Mankiw and Miron (1991)).

There are two dimensions to thinking about the impact on a consumer of these uncertainties and their variations. One dimension is the degree of intertemporal substitution in preferences, and so the ease of adjustment of spending plans. The other is the degree of intertemporal smoothing of abilities to spend. The latter reflects both opportunities and proclivities to smooth.

At the level of individual commodities intertemporal substitution varies a great deal. Delaying food and water is different from delaying a vacation. Delaying payment of a

---

[32] I know of no data, but it seems likely that disproportionately, jobs end at the end of the work week and the work day, with a complementary structure for beginnings.

bill subject to a small late payment charge is different from a late payment resulting in foreclosure. And preferences are not intertemporally additive – attitudes to delay in both meals and vacations depend on how recently one has eaten or had a vacation.

We expect people to plan adequately over the course of a day (although the advent of ATMs is very welcome for the decrease in the need for such planning (and in the cost of inadequate planning)). We expect adults to plan adequately over a week or a month, although differences in frequencies of wage payments suggest that some people think some people are not good at such planning. Even academic economists tend to have their nine month salaries spread (evenly in nominal terms) over twelve months. And Christmas bonuses may reflect a similar view on the ability of people to plan their spending. We don't expect people to plan well over a lifetime.[33]

We are interested in modeling economic equilibrium for both positive and normative reasons. These lectures have focused on the positive. As a brief aside, we would expect different cases for smoothing fluctuations at different frequencies. The fluctuations have different causes and so reflect different tradeoffs between smoothing and bearing fluctuations. People feel differently about day and night, a feeling that would put a sizable cost to a government mandate that smoothed production and sales over the course of the day. People appear to want a weekend, preferring a bunching of leisure time on a daily scale to uniform days. At a longer scale the same is true for vacations – some opportunities just require longer non-work periods. Summer is different from winter as a time for vacation as well as in terms of costs of some production activities. Christmas might have been located at another time, but people seem to like concentrating expenditures, although pressures to conform may make the Christmas demand increase as large as it is. Thus the central issue of business cycles may not be how it is

---

[33] That individuals are not good at smoothing underlies the logic of the compulsion in social insurance systems that provide retirement income (Diamond (1977)).

different from seasonal cycles in patterns of prices and quantities as much as what causes it. If the prime cause is interruption in the income/expenditure flow mechanism, then smoothing of the job-loss risks and job-finding opportunities may involve a different tradeoff at this frequency. That is, a temporary tax cut during a recession seems very different from a temporary tax increase in December.

It is natural to talk about fluctuations in terms of smoothing, but smoothing may not be the right vocabulary. Filling Okun gaps results in a smoother economy, but the gain in the average, not the decrease in the variance may be the central issue. Once one starts to think about short-run unemployment–inflation tradeoffs, some of the variance focus returns to the discussion of when and how to respond to inflationary pressures.

Long run

The focus of this lecture has been the atemporal short-run model. As with a single industry, it is also the case that explicit modeling in time has relevance for the atemporal long-run model. I have not explored that issue, but let me just mark it with another quote from Malinvaud:

> I shall raise the following question: when we move from the neoclassical model of flexible prices to a model with fixed prices and from a slowly moving state to one in which autonomous demand erratically varies, should we not revise the price structure that will prevail on average in the long run in the direction of higher prices and lower wage rates? (1977, p. 98)

That is, recognizing cycles and their effects on rates of return will necessarily revise our theories of the long-run determination of the rate of return and of wages.

Similarly, as noted by Paul Samuelson and Robert Solow (1960), stabilizing an economy affects the mix of inflation and unemployment responses to both shocks and policy actions.

Research agenda

These lectures reflect my attempt to think about the behavior of an economy over time, a topic which, as Marshall said, is difficult. They also reflect my attempt to think coherently about micro and macro. In part, the lectures are stimulated by the curious split between the model that seems most useful in describing the short-run behavior of economies and the models on which macro research currently is concentrated. My belief is that this split comes from the difficulty of finding good research questions relating to the ISLM model and referring to the entire economy. That is, there is interesting research about pieces of explicit-time models that relate to the ISLM perspective and there is research about models of the entire economy that are basically inconsistent with that perspective. My own attempts to model the circular flow of money and goods in a way that would enhance understanding of the ISLM model have been severely limited in what they could accomplish. I would like to think that the limitations come primarily from the difficulty of the questions being researched, the difficulty in having purchasing power determination and pricing behavior happening simultaneously in an explicit-time model.

Ex post, there is little point in research that does not work; little gain from research on questions that were too hard. But it is important not to confuse the research approaches that seem most fruitful with the picture of the economy that seems most reliable. And our current research choices should not block our view of long-run research needs. It seems important to develop models where both price adjustment and determination of the command over purchasing power play out over real time. This seems to me the route to an integrated economics.

REFERENCES

Ainslie, George, 1992, *Picoeconomics: The Strategic Interaction of Successive Motivational States within the Person*, Cambridge: Cambridge University Press.

Arrow, Kenneth J. and F. H. Hahn, 1971, *General Competitive Analysis*, San Francisco: Holden-Day.

Axell, Bo, 1977, "Search Market Equilibrium," *Scandinavian Journal of Economics*, 79: 20–40.

Barro, Robert, 1990, *Macroeconomics*, New York: John Wiley and Sons.

Barro, Robert and Herschel Grossman, 1976, *Money, Employment and Inflation*, Cambridge: Cambridge University Press.

Barsky, Robert B. and Jeffrey A. Miron, 1989, "The Seasonal Cycle and the Business Cycle," *Journal of Political Economy*, 97 (3): 503–32.

Beaulieu, J. Joseph, Jeffrey K. MacKie-Mason, and Jeffrey A. Miron, 1992, "Why Do Countries and Industries with Large Seasonal Cycles Also Have Large Business Cycles?" *Quarterly Journal of Economics*, 107: 621–56.

Beaulieu, J. Joseph and Jeffrey A. Miron, 1990, "The Seasonal Cycle in U.S. Manufacturing," NBER Working Paper 3450.

1992, "A Cross Country Comparison of Seasonal Cycles and Business Cycles," *Economic Journal*, 102: 772–88.

Bénabou, Roland, 1988, "Search, Price Setting and Inflation," *Review of Economic Studies*, 55: 353–73.

1989, "Optimal Price Dynamics and Speculation with a Storable Good," *Econometrica*, 57 (1): 41–80.

1992a, "Inflation and Efficiency in Search Markets," *Review of Economic Studies*, 59: 299–329.

1992b, "Inflation and Markups: Theories and Evidence from the Retail Trade Sector," *European Economic Review*, 36: 566–74.

1993, "Search Market Equilibrium, Bilateral Heterogeneity, and Repeat Purchases," *Journal of Economic Theory*, 60 (1): 140–58.

References

Benassy, Jean-Pascal, 1982, *The Economics of Market Disequilibrium*, New York: Academic Press.

Bernanke, Ben, 1981, "Bankruptcy, Liquidity, and Recession," *American Economic Review Papers and Proceedings*, 71: 155–9.

1983, "Nonmonetary Effects of the Financial Crisis in the Propagation of the Great Depression," *American Economic Review*, 73 (3): 257–76.

Bernanke, Ben and Mark Gertler, 1990, "Financial Fragility and Economic Performance," *Quarterly Journal of Economics*, 105: (1): 87–114.

Bils, Mark, 1987, "The Cyclical Behavior of Marginal Cost and Price," *American Economic Review*, 77 (5): 838–57.

Blanchard, Olivier Jean, 1983, "Price Asynchronization and Price Level Inertia," in Rudiger Dornbusch and Mario Henrique Simonsen (eds.), *Inflation, Debt, and Indexation*, Cambridge MA: MIT Press.

Blanchard, Olivier Jean and Peter Diamond, 1989, "The Beveridge Curve," *Brookings Papers on Economic Activity*, 1: 1–76.

1990a, "The Cyclical Behavior of the Gross Flows of U.S. Workers," *Brookings Papers on Economic Activity*, 2: 85–155.

1990b, "The Aggregate Matching Function," in P. Diamond (ed.), *Growth/Productivity/Unemployment Essays to Celebrate Bob Solow's Birthday*, Cambridge MA: MIT Press.

Blanchard, Olivier Jean and Stanley Fischer, 1989, *Lectures on Macroeconomics*, Cambridge MA: MIT Press.

Blanchard, Olivier Jean and Lawrence F. Katz, 1992, "Regional Evolutions," *Brookings Papers on Economic Activity*, 1: 1–75.

Blanchard, Olivier Jean and Lawrence Summers, 1986, "Hysteresis and the European Unemployment Problem," in Olivier Jean Blanchard and Stanley Fischer (eds.), *NBER Macroeconomics Annual*, Cambridge MA: MIT Press, pp. 15–78.

Blinder, Alan S., 1992, "On Sticky Prices: Academic Theories Meet the Real World," unpublished, prepared for NBER Conference on Monetary Policy.

Brown, F. E. and A. R. Oxenfeldt, 1972, *Misperceptions of Economic Phenomena*, New York: Sperr and Douth.

Burdett, Kenneth and Kenneth Judd, 1983, "Equilibrium Price Dispersion," *Econometrica*, 51: 955–69.

Butters, Gerard, 1977, "Equilibrium Distributions of Sales and

References

Advertising Prices," *Review of Economic Studies*, 44: 467–91.

Caballero, Ricardo, 1989, "Time Dependent Rules, Aggregate Stickiness, and Information Externalities," Columbia DP 428.

Caballero, Ricardo and Eduardo Engel, 1991, "Dynamic (S,s) Economies," *Econometrica*, 59, (6): 1659–86.

1992, "Heterogeneity and Output Fluctuations in a Dynamic Menu Cost Economy," *Review of Economic Studies*, 60: 95–120.

Caballero, Ricardo J. and Mohamad L. Hammour, forthcoming, "The Cleansing Effect of Recessions," *American Economic Review*.

Calvo, Guillermo, 1983, "Staggered Prices in a Utility-Maximizing Framework," *Journal of Monetary Economics*, 12 (3): 383–98.

Caplin, Andrew and John Leahy, 1991, "State-Dependent Pricing and the Dynamics of Money and Output," *Quarterly Journal of Economics*, 106: 683–708.

Caplin, Andrew and Daniel Spulber 1987, "Menu Costs and the Neutrality of Money," *Quarterly Journal of Economics*, 102 (4): 703–26.

Caplin, Andrew, Charles Freeman, and Joseph Tracy, 1993, "Collateral Damage: How Refinancing Constraints Exacerbate Regional Recessions," NBER Working Paper 4531.

Carlton, Dennis W., 1986, "The Rigidity of Prices," *American Economic Review*, 76 (4): 637–58.

1989, "The Theory and the Facts of How Markets Clear: Is Industrial Organization Valuable for Understanding Macroeconomics?" in R. Schmalensee and R. Willig (eds.), *Handbook of Industrial Organization*, vol. I, Elsevier.

Cecchetti, Stephen G., 1986, "The Frequency of Price Adjustment: A Study of Newsstand Prices of Magazines," *Journal of Econometrics*, 31 (3): 255–74.

Christiano, Lawrence J. and Eichenbaum, Martin, 1992a, "Liquidity Effects and the Monetary Transmission Mechanism," *American Economic Review*, 82 (2): 346–53.

1992b, "Liquidity Effects, Monetary Policy and the Business Cycle," Discussion Paper 70, Institute for Empirical Macroeconomics, Federal Reserve Bank of Minneapolis.

Clower, Robert W., 1967, "A Reconsideration of the Microfoundations of Monetary Theory," *Western Economic Journal*, 6: 1–9.

Davis, Steven J. and John Haltiwanger, 1990, "Gross Job Creation

References

and Destruction: Microeconomic Evidence and Macroeconomic Implications," in Olivier Jean Blanchard and Stanley Fischer (eds.), *NBER Macroeconomics Annual*, Cambridge MA: MIT Press, pp. 123–68.

1992, "Gross Job Creation, Gross Job Destruction and Employment Reallocation," *Quarterly Journal of Economics*, 107: 819–63.

Debreu, Gerard, 1959, *Theory of Value*, New York: Wiley.

Diamond, Douglas and Philip Dybvig, 1983, "Bank Runs, Deposit Insurance and Liquidity," *Journal of Political Economy*, 91: 401–19.

Diamond, Peter A., 1965, "National Debt in a Neoclassical Growth Model," *American Economic Review*, 55, 1126–50.

1967, "The Role of a Stock Market in a General Equilibrium Model with Technological Uncertainty," *American Economic Review*, 57: 759–73.

1971, "A Model of Price Adjustment," *Journal of Economic Theory*, 3: 156–68.

1977, "A Framework for Social Security Analysis," *Journal of Public Economics*, 8: 275–98.

1982, "Aggregate Demand Management in Search Equilibrium," *Journal of Political Economy*, 90 (5): 881–94.

1984a, "Money in Search Equilibrium," *Econometrica*, 52 (1) (January): 1–20.

1984b, *A Search-Equilibrium Approach to the Micro Foundations of Macroeconomics, The 1982 Wicksell Lectures*, Cambridge MA: MIT Press.

1987, "Consumer Differences and Prices in a Search Model," *Quarterly Journal of Economics*, 102: 429–36.

1990, "Pairwise Credit in Search Equilibrium," *Quarterly Journal of Economics*, 105: 285–319.

1991, "Search, Sticky Prices and Inflation with Consumer Differences," unpublished, MIT.

1993, "Search, Sticky Prices, and Inflation," *Review of Economic Studies*, 60: 53–68.

1994, "Integrating Allocation and Stabilization Budgets," in J. Quigley and E. Smolensky (eds.), *Modern Public Finance*, Cambridge MA: Harvard University Press.

Diamond, Peter A. and Leonardo Felli, 1990, "Search, Sticky Prices and Deflation," unpublished, MIT.

Diamond, Peter A. and Drew Fudenberg, 1989, "Rational Expectations Business Cycles in Search Equilibrium," *Journal of Political Economy*, 97: 606–19; correction, *Journal of Political Economy*, 99 (1) (1991): 218–19.

References

Diamond, Peter A. and James A. Mirrlees, 1971, "Optimal Taxation and Public Production, I: Production Efficiency and II: Tax Rules," *American Economic Review*, 61: 8–27 and 261–78.

Diamond, Peter A. and Menahem E. Yaari, 1972, "Implications of the Theory of Rationing for Consumer Choice under Uncertainty," *American Economic Review*, 62 (3) (June): 333–43.

Diamond, Peter A. and Joel Yellin, 1985, "The Distribution of Inventory Holdings in a Pure Exchange Barter Search Economy," *Econometrica*, 53 (2) (March): 409–32.

1987, "Pricing and the Distribution of Money Holdings in a Search Economy," in W. Barnett and K. Singleton (eds.), *New Approaches to Monetary Economics*, vol. II, Cambridge: Cambridge University Press, pp. 311–24.

1990, "Inventories and Money Holdings in Search Equilibrium," *Econometrica*, 58 (4) (July): 929–50.

Dixit, Avinash and Robert Pindyck, 1994, *Investment under Uncertainty*, Princeton: Princeton University Press.

Dixit, Avinash and Rafael Rob, 1991, "Switching Costs, Sectoral Adjustments and the Welfare-relevance of Pecuniary Externalities," CARESS WP 91–30, University of Pennsylvania.

Domowitz, Ian, R. Glenn Hubbard and Bruce C. Petersen, 1988, "Market Structure and Cyclical Fluctuations in U.S. Manufacturing," *Review of Economics and Statistics*, 70 (1): 55–66.

Dornbusch, Rudiger and Stanley Fischer, 1994, *Macroeconomics*, 6th edition, New York: McGraw-Hill.

Drèze, Jacques, 1974, "Investment under Private Ownership: Optimality, Equilibrium and Stability," in J. Drèze (ed.), *Allocation under Uncertainty: Equilibrium and Optimality*, New York: Macmillan.

Dunne, Timothy, Mark J. Roberts, and Larry Samuelson, 1989, "Plant Turnover and Gross Employment Flows in the U.S. Manufacturing Sector," *Journal of Labor Economics*, 7 (1): 48–71.

Eatwell, John, Murray Milgate, and Peter Newman (eds.), 1987, *The New Palgrave, A Dictionary of Economics*, London: Macmillan.

Farrell, Joseph and Garth Saloner, 1985, "Standardization, Compatibility, and Innovation," *Rand Journal of Economics*, 16: 70–83.

Fischer, Stanley, 1977, "Long Term Contracts, Rational Expecta-

References

tions and the Optimal Money Supply," *Journal of Political Economy*, 85 (1): 191–206.

Fisher, Irving, 1933, "The Debt-Deflation Theory of Great Depressions," *Econometrica*, 1: 337–57.

Forbes, 151(4) (February 15, 1993).

Frankel, David, 1994, "Search with Telephones," unpublished, MIT.

Friedman, Benjamin M. and Mark J. Warshawsky, 1990, "The Cost of Annuities: Implications for Saving Behavior and Bequests," *Quarterly Journal of Economics*, 105 (1): 135–54.

Geanakoplos, John and Heraklis Polemarchakis, 1986, "Existence, Regularity, and Constrained Suboptimality of Competitive Allocations when the Asset Market is Incomplete," in W. Heller, R. Starr, and D. Starrett (eds.), *Essays in Honor of Kenneth Arrow*, Cambridge: Cambridge University Press, vol. 3, pp. 65–95.

Geanakoplos, John, M. Magill, M. Quinzii, and J. Drèze, 1990, "Generic Inefficiency of Stock Market Equilibria," *Journal of Mathematical Economics*, 19: 113–51.

Gertler, Mark, 1988, "Financial Structure and Aggregate Activity: An Overview," *Journal of Money, Credit and Banking*, 20: 559–88.

Gertler, Mark and Simon Gilchrist, 1993, "The Role of Credit Market Imperfections in the Monetary Transmission Mechanism: Arguments and Evidence," *Scandinavian Journal of Economics*, 95: 43–64.

Gertler, Mark and R. Glenn Hubbard, 1988, "Financial Factors in Business Fluctuations," in *Financial Market Volatility*, A Symposium Sponsored by the Federal Reserve Bank of Kansas City, Jackson Hole, Wyoming, August 17–19.

Gordon, Robert J., 1981, "Output Fluctuations and Gradual Price Adjustment," *Journal of Economic Literature*, 19 (2): 493–531.

Grandmont, Jean-Michel, 1983, *Money and Value*, Cambridge: Cambridge University Press.

1988, *Temporary Equilibrium: Selected Readings*, San Diego: Academic Press.

1992, "Expectations Driven Nonlinear Business Cycles," CFDP 1022, Yale.

Grandmont, Jean-Michel and Guy Laroque, 1976, "Temporary Keynesian Equilibrium," *Review of Economic Studies*, 43: 53–67.

Greenwald, Bruce and Joseph Stiglitz, 1993, "New and Old Keynesians," *Journal of Economic Perspectives*, 7 (1): 23–44.

References

Grossman, Sanford and Laurence Weiss, 1983, "A Transactions-Based Model of the Monetary Transmission Mechanism," *American Economic Review*, 73 (5): 871–80.

Hahn, Frank, 1984, *Equilibrium and Macroeconomics*, Cambridge MA: MIT Press.

Hall, Robert E., 1991, *Booms and Recessions in a Noisy Economy*, Yale University Press.

Hall, Robert E. and John B. Taylor, 1991, *Macroeconomics*, New York: W.W. Norton and Company.

Haltiwanger, John and Michael Waldman, 1991, "Responders versus Non-responders: A New Perspective on Heterogeneity," *Economic Journal*, 101: 1085–102.

Hansson, Björn A., 1982, *The Stockholm School and the Development of Dynamic Method*, London: Croom Helm.

1987, "Stockholm School," in John Eatwell, Murray Milgate, and Peter Newman (eds.), *The New Palgrave, A Dictionary of Economics*, vol. IV, London: Macmillan, 503–06.

1991, "The Stockholm School and the Development of Dynamic Method," in Bo Sandelin (ed.), *The History of Swedish Economic Thought*, London: Routledge, pp. 214–24.

Hart, Oliver, 1975, "On the Optimality of Equilibrium When the Market Structure is Incomplete," *Journal of Economic Theory*, 11: 418–43.

1985, "Monopolistic Competition in the Spirit of Chamberlin: A General Model," *Review of Economic Studies*, 52: 529–46.

Hellwig, Martin F., 1993, "The Conceptual Structure of Macroeconomic Models: I. The Income Equation," WWZ Discussion Paper 9308, Basel.

Hicks, J. R., 1937, "Mr. Keynes and the 'Classics': A Suggested Interpretation," *Econometrica*, 5: 147–59.

1946, *Value and Capital*, second edition, Oxford: Clarendon Press.

Jovanovic, Boyan, 1982, "Selection and the Evolution of Industry," *Econometrica*, 50 (3): 649–70.

Kahneman, Daniel, Jack L. Knetsch, and Richard H. Thaler (1986), "Fairness as a Constraint on Profit Seeking: Entitlements in the Market," *American Economic Review*, 76: 728–41.

Kashyap, Anil K., 1990, "Sticky Prices: New Evidence from Retail Catalogues," Finance and Economics Discussion Paper 112, Federal Reserve Board.

Katz, Michael L. and Carl Shapiro, 1986, "Technology Adoption

References

in the Presence of Network Externalities," *Journal of Political Economy*, 94: 822–41.

King, Robert G., 1993, "Will the New Keynesian Macroeconomics Resurrect the IS–LM Model?" *Journal of Economic Perspectives*, 7 (1): 67–82.

Kiyotaki, Nobuhiro and John Moore, 1993, "Credit Cycles," unpublished paper presented at the Econometric Society Meetings, Boston, June, 1993.

Koelin, Kenneth and Mark Rush, 1990, "Rigid Prices and Flexible Products," Working Paper 90–1, University of Florida.

Kohn, Meir, 1981, "In Defence of the Finance Constraint," *Economic Inquiry*, 19: 177–95.

1983, "Aggregate Demand in the Neoclassical Theory of the Business Cycle," unpublished, Dartmouth College.

Kohn, Meir and Sho-Chieh Tsiang, 1988, *Finance Constraints and Economic Activity*, Oxford: Oxford University Press.

Koopmans, Tjalling, 1942, "The Dynamics of Inflation," *Review of Economics and Statistics*, 24: 53–65.

Kreps, David M., 1990, *A Course in Microeconomic Theory*, Princeton: Princeton University Press.

Kydland, Finn and Edward Prescott, 1982, "Time to Build and Aggregate Fluctuations," *Econometrica*, 50 (6): 1345–70.

Lazear, Edward P., 1986, "Retail Pricing and Clearance Sales," *American Economic Review*, 76 (2): 14–32.

Lindahl, Erik, 1939, *Studies in the Theory of Money and Capital*, New York: Farrar and Rinehart.

Lippman, S. A. and R. P. Rumelt, 1982, "Uncertain Imitability: An Analysis of Interfirm Differences in Efficiency under Competition," *Bell Journal of Economics*, 13 (2): 418–38.

Loewenstein, George and Jon Elster, 1992, *Choice Over Time*, New York: The Russell Sage Foundation.

Lucas, Robert E., Jr, 1990, "Liquidity and Interest Rates," *Journal of Economic Theory*, 50 (2): 237–64.

Lucas, Robert E., Jr and Edward Prescott, 1974, "Equilibrium Search and Unemployment," *Journal of Economic Theory*, 7: 188–209.

Lucas, Robert E., Jr and Michael Woodford, 1993, "Real Effects of Monetary Shocks in an Economy with Sequential Purchases," NBER Working Paper 4250.

Lundberg, Erik, 1937, *Studies in the Theory of Economic Expansion*, London: P.S. King & Son.

Machlup, Fritz, 1959, "Statics and Dynamics: Kaleidoscope Words," *Southern Economic Journal*, 26: 2, reprinted in

References

1991, *Economic Semantics*, New Brunswick: Transaction Publishers.

Malinvaud, Edmond, 1977, *The Theory of Unemployment Reconsidered*, Oxford: Basil Blackwell.

Mankiw, N. Gregory, 1992, *Macroeconomics*, New York: Worth Publishers.

Mankiw, N. Gregory and Jeffrey A. Miron, 1991, "Should the Fed Smooth Interest Rates? The Case of Seasonal Monetary Policy," *Carnegie-Rochester Conference Series on Public Policy*, 34: 41–69.

Mankiw, N. Gregory and David Romer, 1991, *New Keynesian Economics, Volume 1: Imperfect Competition and Sticky Prices, Volume 2: Coordination Failures and Real Rigidities*, Cambridge MA: MIT Press.

Marshall, Alfred, 1948, *Principles of Economics*, eighth edition, New York: The Macmillan Company.

McCormick, Barry, 1991, *Unemployment Structure and the Unemployment Puzzle*, London: Employment Institute.

Miron, Jeffrey A., 1994, "The Economics of Seasonal Cycles," in C. Sims (ed.), *Advances in Econometrics: Sixth World Congress*, vol. I, Cambridge: Cambridge University Press.

Mortensen, Dale, 1978, "Specific Capital, Bargaining, and Labor Turnover," *Bell Journal of Economics*, 9 (2): 572–86.

Nagle, Thomas T. and Kenneth Novak, 1988, "The Roles of Segmentation and Awareness in Explaining Variations in Price Markups," in Timothy M. Devinney (ed.), *Issues in Pricing*, Lexington, MA: Lexington Books.

Pashigian, B. Peter, 1988, "Demand Uncertainty and Sales: A Study of Fashion and Markdown Pricing," *American Economic Review*, 78 (5): 936–53.

Pashigian, B. Peter and Brian Bowen, 1991, "Why Are Products Sold on Sale? Explanations of Pricing Regularities," *Quarterly Journal of Economics*, 106 (4): 1015–38.

1992, "Why Has the Pricing of New Cars Changed?" unpublished, University of Chicago.

Phelps, Edmund S., 1970, *Microeconomic Foundations of Inflation and Employment Theory*, New York: Norton.

Phelps, Edmund S. and Sidney G. Winter, Jr, 1970, "Optimal Price Policy under Atomistic Competition," in E. S. Phelps (ed.), *Microeconomic Foundations of Inflation and Employment Theory*, New York: Norton.

Pratt, John, David Wise, and Richard Zeckhauser, 1979, "Price Differences in Almost Competitive Markets," *Quarterly Journal of Economics*, 93: 189–212.

References

Prescott, Edward C., 1975, "Efficiency of the Natural Rate,"
   Journal of Political Economy, 83: 1229–36.
   1986, "Theory Ahead of Business Cycle Measurement,"
   Federal Reserve Bank of Minneapolis, *Quarterly Review*, 10
   (4): 9–22.
   1991, "Real Business Cycle Theory: What Have We Learned?"
   Revista de Análisis Económico, 6 (2): 3–19.
Ramsey, Frank, 1928, "A Mathematical Theory of Saving,"
   Economic Journal, 38: 543–59.
Reinganum, Jennifer F., 1979, "A Simple Model of Equilibrium
   Price Dispersion," *Journal of Political Economy*, 87: 851–8.
Rob, Rafael, 1985, "Equilibrium Price Distributions," *Review of
   Economic Studies*, 52: 487–504.
Robertson, Sir Dennis, 1926, *Banking Policy and the Price Level*,
   1989 reprint, Fairfield, New Jersey: Augustus M. Kelley.
   1959, *Lectures on Economic Principles, Volume III*, London:
   Staples Press.
Romer, Christina D. and David H. Romer, 1989, "Does Monetary
   Policy Matter? A New Test in the Spirit of Friedman and
   Schwartz," *NBER Macroeconomics Annual*, 4: 121–70.
Romer, David, 1987, "The Monetary Transmission Mechanism
   in a General Equilibrium Version of the Baumol–Tobin
   Model," *Journal of Monetary Economics*, 20: 105–22.
Rotemberg, Julio, 1983, "A Monetary Equilibrium Model with
   Transactions Costs," *Journal of Political Economy*, 92 (2):
   40–58.
   1988, "Rationing in Centrally Planned Economies," MIT
   Working Paper 2024.
Rotemberg, Julio J. and Garth Saloner, 1986, "A Supergame-
   Theoretic Model of Price Wars during Booms," *American
   Economic Review*, 76: 390–407.
Rotemberg, Julio J. and Michael Woodford, 1991, "Counter-
   cyclical Markups," in Olivier Jean Blanchard and Stanley
   Fischer (eds.), *NBER Macroeconomics Annual*, Cambridge
   MA: MIT Press.
Salop, Steven C., 1979, "Monopolistic Competition with Outside
   Goods," *Bell Journal of Economics*, 10: 141–56.
Salop, Steven C. and Joseph Stiglitz, 1977, "Bargains and Ripoffs:
   A Model of Monopolistically Competitive Price Dispersion,"
   Review of Economic Studies, 44: 493–510.
Samuelson, Paul A., 1947, *Foundations of Economic Analysis*,
   Cambridge MA: Harvard University Press.
Samuelson, Paul A. and Robert M. Solow, 1960, "Analytic

References

Aspects of Anti-Inflation Policy," *American Economic Review*, 50 (2): 177–94.

Sargent, Thomas J., 1987, *Dynamic Macroeconomic Theory*, Cambridge MA: Harvard University Press.

Schelling, Thomas, 1984, "Self Command in Practice, in Policy and in a Theory of Rational Thought," *American Economic Review*, 74 (2): 1–11.

Shafir, Eldar, Peter Diamond, and Amos Tversky, 1992, "On Money Illusion," unpublished, MIT.

Sheshinski, Eytan and Yoram Weiss, 1993, *Optimal Pricing, Inflation, and the Cost of Price Adjustment*, Cambridge MA: MIT Press.

Shi, Shouyong, 1992, "Money and Prices: A Model of Search and Bargaining," unpublished, University of Windsor.

Shilony, Yuval, 1977, "Mixed Pricing in Oligopoly," *Journal of Economic Theory*, 14: 373–88.

Solow, Andrew R., 1991, "Is There A Global Warming Problem?" in R. Dornbusch and J. Poterba (eds.), *Global Warming: Economic Policy Responses*, Cambridge MA: MIT Press, pp. 7–28.

Stigler, George and James Kindahl, 1970, *The Behavior of Industrial Prices*, NBER General Series No. 90, New York: Columbia University Press.

Strotz, Robert H., 1955, "Myopia and Inconsistency in Dynamic Utility Maximization," *Review of Economic Studies*, 23: 165–80.

Taylor, John, 1979, "Staggered Price Setting in a Macro Model," *American Economic Review*, 69 (2): 108–13.

Tirole, Jean, 1988, *The Theory of Industrial Organization*, Cambridge MA: MIT Press.

Tobin, James, 1972, "Inflation and Unemployment," *American Economic Review*, 62 (1): 1–18.

Trejos, Alberto and Randall Wright, 1993, "Search, Bargaining, Money and Prices," CARESS WP 93–13, University of Pennsylvania.

Varian, Hal R., 1980, "A Model of Sales," *American Economic Review*, 70 (4): 651–9.

Warner, Elizabeth J. and Robert B. Barsky, 1993, "The Timing and Magnitude of Retail Store Markdowns with Reference to Weekends and Holidays," unpublished, University of Michigan.

Wheaton, William, 1990, "Vacancy, Search, and Prices in a Housing Market Matching Model," *Journal of Political Economy*, 98 (6): 1270–92.

References

White, James J. and Frank W. Munger, Jr, 1971, "Consumer Sensitivity to Interest Rates: An Empirical Study of New Car Buyers and Auto Loans," *Michigan Law Review*, 69: 1204–58.

Wilde, Louis, 1977, "Labor Market Equilibrium under Non-sequential Search," *Journal of Economic Theory*, 16: 373–93.

Wilde, Louis and Alan Schwartz, 1979, "Equilibrium Comparison Shopping," *Review of Economic Studies*, 46: 543–54.

Woodford, Michael, 1990, "Optimal Monetary Policy in an Economy with Sequential Service of Buyers," unpublished, University of Chicago.

INDEX OF NAMES

Index of names

INDEX OF SUBJECTS